Pacifiers, Blankets, Bottles, and Thumbs

WHAT PARENTS SHOULD KNOW ABOUT STARTING AND STOPPING

Mark L. Brenner

A FIRESIDE BOOK
Published by Simon & Schuster
New York   London   Toronto   Sydney

FIRESIDE
Rockefeller Center
1230 Avenue of the Americas
New York, NY 10020

FIRESIDE and colophon are registered trademarks
of Simon & Schuster, Inc.

Designed by Chris Welch

Manufactured in the United States of America

2 4 6 8 10 9 7 5 3 1

Library of Congress Cataloging-in-Publication Data
Brenner, Mark L., 1950–
Pacifiers, blankets, bottles, and thumbs : what parents should know
about starting and stopping / Mark L. Brenner.
p. cm.
"A Fireside book."
Includes bibliographical references and index.
1. Child psychology. 2. Transitional objects (Psychology) 3. Attachment
behavior in children. 4. Regression (Psychology) 5. Habit breaking. I. Title.

HQ772.B684 2004
305.231—dc22   2003069653

ISBN 0-7432-4334-X

For information regarding special discounts for bulk purchases,
please contact Simon & Schuster Special Sales at 1-800-456-6798
or business@simonandschuster.com.

for my max and merrill

"The Big Sissy"

One summer evening during a violent thunderstorm, a mother was tucking her small boy into bed. She was about to turn off the light when he asked with a tremor in his voice, "Mommy, will you sleep with me tonight?"

The mother smiled and gave him a reassuring hug. "I can't, dear," she said. "I have to sleep in Daddy's room." A long silence was broken with a little voice saying . . . "The big sissy."

—*Anonymous*

Contents

A Note About the Use of Pronouns

Unfortunately, the English language has no neutral singular pronoun and causes an author to assign a gender with *he* or *she*. To prevent the use of only one pronoun, I have randomly alternated between the use of *he* and *she*. However, please understand it is my intention that you have your own child in mind as you come across examples that fit your own child's behavior.

Acknowledgments

In the end, like most projects, it comes down to people. In my case, and at the top of the list, are the children. I am always humbled by how much they see and know. I remain grateful to all of the children and their families with whom I've had the privilege of working.

To my beautiful wife, my first love and my first editor.

To my mother for her unflinching believing.

This book is about giving, not so much about things, but understanding. A very special thank-you to Rae and Jack Gindi, who set the standard for giving and an unequivocating belief in goodness.

What Are Transitional Objects?

"*I see here, Walters, you started with the firm when you were very young.*"

Sometimes we need to hold on, so later we can let go.

—MARK L. BRENNER

It doesn't take long to realize that the questions we have about our child's behavior often lead us to direct discoveries about our own behavior. Jerry, a successful thirty-six-year-old dentist and father of two, getting ready to go to the gym, yells out to his wife, "Honey, where's my favorite workout shirt?" He says it with a fierce attachment, as though the workout will not be as good without that special T-shirt. At the same time, four-year-old Tommy, on his way to the supermarket with Mom, is searching frantically at the last minute for his little teddy bear. A closer look at both attachments reveals the same expectation: a feeling of well-being.

In the 1950s, no one understood this more than the pioneering British pediatrician and child psychiatrist Donald W. Winnicott. Winnicott developed one of the most famous *transitional*-object concepts, focusing on familiar, inanimate objects that children use to stave off anxiety during times of stress. Anxiety is an overwhelming feeling of *uncertainty,* a general feeling that something either is wrong or will go wrong, defined as that all-too-familiar butterfly feeling in our stomach that surfaces even throughout adulthood when our secure base is threatened.

With an infant-turned-toddler, the transitional object often starts acquiring importance when he emerges from the symbiotic relationship and begins to distinguish between himself and his mother. Transitional objects are the first "not-me" possessions of the infant. Later, the object can represent both himself and his mother; it can remind him of his mother's look, touch, or smell and provide a means by which he can take that with him. It can remain under his *control* while Mom is absent. Learning to use a transitional object is an *important* experience for a child as he tries to increase independence and mastery.

One mother remembers her early reaction to her child's first experience this way: *When my first child was born in 1997, I was proud that she didn't seem to need anything soft and cuddly—until I noticed a bald patch on the side of her head. She'd been pulling out her hair to snuggle with. I cut up a soft old jumper and she happily transferred to that, dropping it and her thumb at the same time when she was four.*

If a natural attachment to the mother or father is *not* present in a child's life, a child may become more prone to attachment with an object as an extension of herself. In all cases, any personal possession can function as a transitional object: it could be a piece of a cloth blanket, a stuffed animal, a doll, a toy, or any other freely chosen object. Whatever it is, the transitional object allows the child to begin to understand and practice developing human relationships in terms of empathy, loyalty, and competency. These object relationships may last much longer than most parents expect.

The transitional object allows the child to begin to understand and practice developing human relationships in terms of empathy, loyalty, and competency.

Still, some children give up their transitional objects or habits quicker (pacifiers and bottles included), while others require a little more help. It should come as no surprise that an attachment to a specific transitional object can develop as early as at six months of age. Generally speaking, attachment objects take on even greater importance to a child when he is about two years old. These freely chosen objects are irresistible to children because, for the most part, they are small, cozy, and "totally predictable." The young child also enjoys having authority over something. In addition to providing extra control, the transitional object helps a child prove his autonomy while at the same time maintain his feelings associated with familiarity. Just as important, between the ages of two and three, children become more independent and develop the necessary skills that allow them to emotionally relate to people *other* than the people most important to them. These freely chosen objects help bridge that independent growth. As a word of caution, a child's transitional object should never be used by the parent as a punishment or reward for behavior. For example, "Janet, if you keep on whining, I'm going to take your horsey away."

As a word of caution, never use a child's transitional object as a punishment or reward for behavior. For example, "Janet, if you keep on whining, I'm going to take your horsey away."

So, when should parents recognize that their child has chosen an object attachment to become an extension of his mother or himself? Essentially, when the child insists that there can be no other substitute for that object. Winnicott suggests six special qualities with which the child must imbue his relationship with that object for it to become a transitional object:

1. The child assumes all rights over the object.
2. The object is freely cuddled, loved, or even mangled.
3. The object must never be changed by anybody, unless by the child himself.
4. The object must survive instinctual loving, hating, and pure aggression the child will show it.
5. The object must seem to the child to give warmth, to move, or to do something that imbues it with personality or reality of its own.
6. The object's fate must be gradually allowed to be disregarded, so that in the years ahead it becomes not so much forgotten as relegated to limbo. This means it is not forgotten and it is not mourned; it just loses its earlier meaning and thereby allows for transition.

Freud originally used the term *object* to mean anything an infant or child directs toward self-satiation. Expanding on Freud, many contemporary theorists also believe the object becomes the focus of relational needs in human development. Such objects can of course include an unlimited number of things to which we form attachments, as well as, in a more maladaptive way, people. Modern object relations theorists, and in particular professor and psychologist Robert Klee of Chestnut Hill College, believes a child makes multiple object attachments, and the developing child's relationship with them are incorporated into a self and as such become one of the building blocks of the self system and personality. In short, understanding object relations is a way to view ourselves in relation to others. That is why *object* relations is a more apt term than human relations: It is important to use the term *object* because it can mean both the human and the inanimate. Each type of object can become uniquely self-serving in how the child (or adult) makes personal use of those projected qualities.

Most parents think of a child as having only one object of attachment. While this may sometimes be true, children more commonly have multiple objects from which they choose at different times for different reasons. Transitional objects are not just for the *big* and obvious, recognizable stages of development such as we see in toddlerhood and childhood. There are subtle transitional objects that a child attaches to, which take place way under the radar of the watchful eye, such as a favorite spoon, cup, or shirt. That is why when a big change in behavior is finally revealed, many parents are surprised! ("Honey, is it just me, or doesn't little Jeremy seem a lot older today?") Pouring cereal, dressing himself more easily, exhibiting fewer mood swings, or talking more comfortably to strangers are indicators of a new transition and a readiness to leave behind old object attachments. Until that time, most children want their transitional object with them for reasons that are not always obvious to a parent. "I want my horsey," Charlie says as he gets ready for a bath. Hanna looks for her special "magic wand" before going to the supermarket with her mother. More obvious is Caroline's need to find her teddy bear at nap time. Danny developed a stronger attachment to his GI Joe combat soldier when his new sister was born. David's new Yugio trading card rarely leaves his pocket. Spontaneously chosen objects whose significance may seem obscure to a parent are keenly understood and played with as part of another transitional day for the child. Such objects are part of little and big moments.

> **There are subtle transitional objects that a child attaches to, which take place way under the radar of the watchful eye, such as a favorite spoon, cup, or shirt.**

So the term *object* is more inclusive for our understanding of how children interact with and maintain their human relationships. Before we limit or disrupt the active play with these transitional objects, parents should first seek to understand their fuller meanings. Habits and/or attachments should always be evaluated in the context of a child's age. For example, a four- or five-year-old still sucking his thumb is very different from a five- or six-year-old carrying around a favorite doll or stuffed animal. It is through our collective attachments, including those with the significant people around us, that we take in parts of them and slowly build a self, which we eventually call personality. Once formed, this blueprint can be modified, but our basic tendency is to seek out the people and object relationships that will reaffirm certain memories from our early childhood. This does not mean our script can't change. However, the more problematic our early experiences were with regard to our object relations, the more rigid and resistant we can become later in life with respect to letting go of things and what we *think* is important. This can manifest in many ways. Adults who were denied the psychological security of a secure base as a child may have a tendency to save everything they acquire in adulthood, including closets filled with worthless junk. Unable to throw anything out, they have an irrational need and an unresolved desire to control their environment.

In the end, it will largely be our early recollections that define and motivate us as adults to reconstruct parts of our past. If we are earnest in our effort to change, we can fulfill our authentic potential. Alfred Adler in 1937 put it this way:

> When rightly understood in relation to the rest of an individual's life, early recollections are found always to have a bearing on the central interests of that person's life. Early recollections give us hints and clues which are most valuable to follow when attempting the task of finding the direction of a person's striving. They are most helpful in revealing what one regards as values to be aimed for and what one senses as dangers to be avoided. They illuminate the origins of the choices in life. The basic attitudes which have guided an individual throughout his life and which prevail, likewise, in his present situation, are reflected in those fragments which he has selected to epitomize his feeling about life, and to cherish in his memory as reminders. He has preserved these as his early recollections.

Pacifiers, Blankets, Bottles, and Thumbs will surprise you, not just because of a new understanding it will give you in recognizing the critical role transitional objects play in the social development of your child, but because of the insights you will gain into how many adults themselves use object attachments to heighten their own feelings of security and well-being. I decided to write this book while giving one of my Parent Fitness Training workshops. I teach parents a six-week plan to improve their *performance* in building up the parent-child relationship. During my introduction to the training and while asking for a show of hands of how many parents had children between the ages of two and seven, one parent interrupted and called out: "I need an instant remedy to help rid my three-year-old daughter of her binky habit!" Over 70 percent of the other parents joined in, telling me they all had the same problem. One particular mom spoke to me as if I were a pharmacist ready to dispense the perfect pill: "I need the cure for getting rid of that *thing* in her mouth—I can't take it anymore!" More noteworthy than her question was her conspicuously high-strung demeanor. Mom was wound up tighter than a ball of rubber bands. As we all found out that evening, so was her daughter. Ready to explode when feeling the slightest anxiety or frustration, her daughter automatically reached for her rubbery piece of plastic to help her calm down.

Parent Fitness Training requires many of the same principles as getting in shape at the gym. One of those key principles, aside from commitment and consistency, is managing expectations. Nothing changes in five minutes except maybe the California weather. It is crucial that parents get a realistic idea of how long it will take for behavior patterns to change. A parent who manages expectations successfully will increase tolerance and patience.

A parent who manages expectations successfully will increase tolerance and patience.

This book will help you acquire the knowledge to manage your expectations more realistically. Imagine deciding one day that you want to lose weight and get in shape, and you hire a trainer. Would you ever say to your trainer, "You think I can drop eighteen pounds and build my abs in three days?" Hardly, yet that is exactly what many parents think *before* following a wise parenting idea. Frustrated, a parent may think, "If it doesn't give me instant results or if it stops working after a few times, I'm going to quit using that idea." By contrast, when working out at the gym, we're willing to wait at least sixty days for changes to take place, but we want our parenting ideas to work in five minutes or we quit!

Invariably, and at different stages of a child's development, a parent may ask, "Is this healthy? Should my son or daughter still be using that or doing that?" Of course, sometimes the behavior is just a stage. Other times, however, it's an early indication of a more serious pattern to come. No child enjoys throwing tantrums and spinning out of control. He first looks to his parent(s) to provide a way back to a secure feeling. If that connection and trust are not available—well, you know the whining reaction and what's to come! The good news is that with a proper understanding of transitional objects and a good plan of intervention and dialogue, you can help your child begin to feel a new kind of well-being. Generally speaking, object attachments are as healthy as any weekly workout at the gym. If the metaphor of going to the gym makes you feel a little guilty because you never go, then substitute your daily trek to Starbucks for that morning cup of vanilla nut. The legendary late cartoonist Charles Schultz reminded us of our need for routine and comfort by giving us the character Linus and revealing this important aspect of the human psyche. In so many of Schultz's *Peanuts* strips, we would watch an anxious Linus clinging to his favorite blanket as he tackled life's difficulties. Transitional objects play a powerful humanizing role in the development of a child. Being on alert and asking the right questions make every parent a wiser one.

Transitional objects play a powerful humanizing role in the development of a child.

For example:

Can television act as a pacifier?
When does a behavior become a habit?
What are the different types of attachments?
How does having these objects help children?
Am I encouraging the behavior by giving in?

Does my child see me with my own form of object attachments?
Am I doing damage letting my two-year-old drink from a bottle?
How long should I let my child carry around his blanket?

Just as children vary in personality and temperament, they differ in the degree of their immediate need for autonomy. Right from birth, some act with a lasting burst of independence, while others seem to always be hanging on to Mom, as if being held in place by a large piece of super Velcro. As intuitive parents, we can sometimes see and feel our young child's need for dependence—masked in irritability or an insatiable need to be rocked, comforted, or held in the arms of a particular parent. This behavior, though exhausting to the parent, may unwittingly be prolonged by the parent who becomes codependent on such closeness. Being needed is a very powerful feeling. A lonely marriage, divorce, and a host of other personal problems are all factors that can foster parent-child codependence. This sends an unmistakable signal that some children will take to mean: "Something must be wrong with me. I'd better stay close to Mommy or Daddy."

Understanding why your child appears to be developing a compulsive attachment to a certain object can provide a window into his unspoken needs. As with all self-defeating behaviors, when it interferes with natural development and human interaction, it is time to examine such behavior more closely, in terms of his degree of withdrawal or shyness. On the other hand, the great majority of young children who love their favorite teddy bears or special toys are well within the healthy limits of feeling attached. Like two old friends who know the best and worst of each other, so goes the transitional object relationship. Untold secrets and the most private feelings can exist between a child and his favorite object. Most experts would agree that children differ to one degree or another in both intensity and attachment to a particular transitional object. On the other hand, of course, some children never develop a fixation for one particular object for any length of time. Nothing should be read into this behavior either.

TWO

The Secure Base

A child's life is like a piece of paper on which
every passerby leaves a mark.

—CHINESE PROVERB

Home sweet home. Intuitively, we all know its deeper meaning. Not surprisingly, the need for a secure base begins well before an infant or toddler selects his favorite little stuffed animal. It's a central aspect of parenting to provide a secure base for a child and, later, adolescent to which he can return at any time for physical and emotional comfort, encouragement, and reassurance. The role of the secure base is, most of the time, to just wait, to be there, to be available, ready to respond when required. When a child with a secure base develops greater emotional and intellectual maturity, he can begin to substitute specific memories for using his objects to strengthen his attachment to Mom, Dad, or family.

> **One of a child's, not to mention an adult's, major goals in life is to feel that he belongs and is significant in his family, his school, and the world at large. If these expectations are met, stability develops.**

One of a child's, as well as an adult's, major drives in life is to feel that he belongs and is significant in his family, his school, and the world at large. If these expectations are met, stability develops. If they're not, a child spends his energy trying to prove that he fits in instead of enjoying normal social interaction. If an individual feels he has achieved a sense of belonging in his family and/or school, then he need not waste precious psychological energy striving to find his place. This can be seen dramatically in the classroom: a child *cannot* concentrate on learning if he is consumed with fitting in. When he is made to feel accepted and part of the larger classroom community, his anxiety level decreases and his attention to staying on task increases. The same dynamics hold true in the family system. Many children get lots of spontaneous hugs and kisses, yet feel invisible and harbor an underlying feeling that they really don't count. Hugs alone do not make a child feel like he counts; a parent's honest acknowledgment in reflecting back how a child is feeling does. As the child psychologist Haim Ginott used to say, "If a child feels right, he acts right!" Poor socialization usually means poor attachment.

In my earlier book, *When No Gets You Nowhere: Teaching Your Toddler Self-Control,* I emphasize the critical importance of recognizing that a child's feelings are at the center of his development and his need to be part of a secure base. The problem begins when parents mistakenly *focus* first on exacting the "right" behavior, or stopping undesirable behavior, and not on *liquidating the negative feelings* motivating those actions in the first place. It is not popular to say, but far too much emphasis over the years has been placed on getting behavioral results at the expense of the real well-being of the child. Children, like adults, will conceal their true feelings and shut down when emotionally dismissed. They begin to create a separate identity for the world to see, while underneath feeling empty and invisible. We know from our own lives that pent-up and repressed feelings just don't go away. If not properly expressed, they will emerge through a host of self-destructive relationship-bearing behaviors. Frustration and feeling misunderstood in any primary relationship will likely bring about a *longer* firestorm of noncompliance, conflict, and codependence. This philosophy is not a license for a child to behave any way he wants. In other words, there is a huge difference between allowing all feelings and allowing all behavior!

Certain everyday scenarios seem to bring out a clingy child's worst fears and send him scurrying for the security of a parent's pant leg or a transitional object. Three- and four-year-olds who have not properly felt a secure base often remain on *ready alert* to any rapid changes, such as visiting new places, last-minute trips, classroom uncertainty, or simple transitioning to a new babysitter. They can be expected to look to their parents and other adults for constant reassurance. In such cases, a transitional object can be a great liaison to help diminish feelings of helplessness, anxiety, or abandonment—though never a substitute for a healthy parent–child relationship.

For children, we supply a secure base by making specific sacrifices unconditionally. Of course, we do not make the child feel guilty about these sacrifices. Threats of abandonment or withdrawal of affection and respect for the child must *never* be acted on, even when he breaks a rule or disappoints us. As we get older we must always be mindful of how our secure base has contributed *(or not)* to our own well-being. Some adults unwisely take for granted their own secure base. It can easily be forgotten how much a spouse, mother, father, or friend has given in creating that secure base. Many adults who become successful later in life or have gone through significant positive changes because of someone's personal influence can selfishly forget, if one is caught up in the ego of success. Cavalier attitudes by others can be emotionally disruptive if gone unchecked. No one likes to be used or taken for granted—this creates buried feelings of resentment and anger that emerge in adult relationships.

The truth is, the feeling of having a secure base is needed all through our lives. We all quietly feel happiest when we know there is a someone somewhere we can return to and feel welcome and taken care of by. The more secure the base is, the more confidently we can move throughout our world. Even in our powerful military, where our strong armies and soldiers protect our great country, each and every heroic soldier knows central command—a secure base—is just a ping away through their GPS tracking gear. It is more than high tech: it is high touch. It encourages fierce independence to complete the mission while at the same time provides a feeling of connectedness.

The secure base encourages healthy attachment. Attachment can take three forms: it can be an emotional bond between two people, between a human and an animal, or between a human and an inanimate object such as a toy, blanket, or favorite shirt. In infants, attachments do not form in both directions at once. Early on, the caretaker-to-infant attachment develops rapidly, usually within the first month of life. The development of the infant-to-caretaker bond develops much more slowly.

In fact, there is little evidence that infants bond to their parent or primary caretaker until somewhere between five and ten months, when stranger anxiety appears. Up to this time, infants are typically happy being held or taken care of by any adult who is reasonably tuned in, gentle, and caring.

Unfortunately, and as an unintentional consequence, our culture makes little distinction between primary care and substitute care. Society places a higher value on a mother's desire for independence from family than her own natural desire for emersed motherhood. We are now experiencing the first generation of women giving birth and raising families who did not have a full-time mother at home during critical periods of their own development. These young women, since they did not experience a secure base of attachment, have no sense of the essential role they play in their children's lives and so do not even question the value and power of substitute care. They accept it as a given that children will thrive away from their mothers. Such is the unforeseen legacy of feminism. Children are being left at younger and younger ages for longer and longer periods of time, and the assumption is that they will thrive. While it is true that these mothers appear to be feeling better about themselves, their children are feeling worse.

There is little evidence that infants bond to their parent or primary caretaker until somewhere between five and ten months, when stranger anxiety appears. Up to this time, infants are typically happy being held or taken care of by any adult who is reasonably tuned in, gentle, and caring.

The need for a secure base and attachment was best demonstrated in the famous 1950s experiment by Harry Harlow. To prove his theory of attachment and comfort bonding, Harlow created "substitute" mothers for two infant Rhesus monkeys. One substitute mother was created of chicken wire and topped with a plastic head that was not very monkeylike. A feeding bottle was placed in its chest so that an infant monkey could nurse. The other substitute mother was similar, except that the chicken-wire body was covered with a soft, furry cloth, and it had no bottle. Surprisingly, the infant monkey paired with the furless "mother" failed to bond with it, even though it was fed only by this substitute mother. In contrast, the other infant monkey did bond to the substitute mother that was covered with soft, furry cloth—even though that mother *never* fed it. Feeding, then, did not seem to promote attachment. Rather, it appeared that the comfort provided by the contact with the soft, furry mother was crucial to promoting attachment. The infant monkey's attachment to the furry mother showed many of the characteristics of normal human attachment. The infant monkeys were comforted by *contact* with the substitute mother. They both clung to her, and when someone tried to separate them from the substitute mother, they ran back to the furry substitute because they were frightened. Harlow's important research suggested that *contact* comfort may be biological and is one of the factors that promotes formation of infant-to-caretaker bonds. This primordial need to feel close shows up throughout our lifelong relationships when we are faced with loneliness, fear, or severe loss.

Newborns do not display a preference for being with their parents or caretakers over other people. Somewhere between five and ten months of age, though, they start to prefer being with their parents or other familiar people, or they may cry when their parents or primary caretakers try to leave them with a stranger. This latter phenomenon is referred to as stranger anxiety. When it appears, we can infer that the child has formed a bond with his familiar caretakers and prefers them above other people. It could be said that the infant has formed his first attachment.

As the infant progresses past the first six months of life toward a sense of self, the mother or primary caretaker gives him an identity and nurtures the roots of personality. In the first few months of life, the infant does not yet distinguish between the inner and outer world, between himself and his mother, but the mother can and does communicate her knowledge to her infant as the infant looks in her face. What comes before looking in any mirror? The mother's face. In other words, the mother's face is the infant's mirror! This is a revelation Bruno Bettelheim, the 1950s child psychologist, brought to the minds of many psychologists and parents. Most mothers would say they believe their newborn is looking up at them, as though their infant sees them as a separate being. Not so. To be sure, the infant has not yet even discovered his own hands and feet. The stage of individuation has not begun. The child's own *feeling* of well-being comes as a result of the mother's facial expression and mood. For the young infant, the mother's face is his own. Her facial expressions, grimaces, and smiles provide clues in helping the child see himself. The infant with a depressed or introverted mother, then, is off to a bad start. At the same time, the mother's initial role is also one of *holding,* giving the infant a secure base from which to begin a more active exploration for his developing capacities for communication and play.

As the infant rapidly develops, his natural development of play is now well under way. Early play is connected with the realities of both *illusion* and *disillusion.* Right at the beginning, shortly after birth, the hungry infant may hallucinate a breast; very near that moment, the sensitive mother, knowing her infant is hungry, responds by providing her breast. The infant has the illusion of unlimited power: he thinks of something, and *bam,* there it is! Likewise, when he is full and satiated, he may play with his mother's breast as an object of fun. However, soon after, there will be inevitable disillusions to deal with, and if the mother does not help her young child to accept these constraints of reality, frustration, leading to a disconnection, may be the unintended consequence. While imaginative play may often not fully resolve the frustration, it is the only medium for a child's natural release. As the infant quickly moves into early toddlerhood, spontaneous free play will remain the subtle antibody to fight off conflict, fear, and anxiety.

The Meaning Behind Play

One of the most natural elements in childhood development is the connection between a child's free play and his playtime use of transitional objects, acquiring a kind of Huckleberry Finn and Harry Potter context to solving the real and imaginary problems of growing up. Winnicott argued that the transitional object is the first manifestation of creative play. He also felt that the transitional object is the prototype of all later relationships between ourselves and others. The power and revelations contained in a child's favorite bear, toy, special dress-up outfit, or newly invented superhero character have great import for that child. To the unobservant parent, it all may just seem like cute play. Look and listen much closer. A child's use of transitional objects runs at full throttle; play for children is the equivalent of what conversations are for adults. Toys can be words for children! A play setting without the typical constraints of adult symbols and furnishings is the natural environment for observing and understanding the real child, who is not stressed by being in a situation in which he is forced to answer questions or behave in a prescribed way. The child who lives with a healthy, secure base is free to experience her play with the full range of what is in her heart and her mind. In play, children interact with toys and other people in ways that will spontaneously include and reflect both past and present-day relationships. Play is how they rehearse new skills and solutions. Too often, parents think of playing with their children as a constant state of teaching: "Look how this is done!" "Look where this goes!" "Do it this way, it works better!" The real secret to revealing a child's heart and building trust is to allow the child to lead the parent in spontaneous play.

> **Too often, parents think of playing with their children as a constant state of teaching: "Look how this is done!" "Look where this goes!" "Do it this way, it works better!" The real secret to revealing a child's heart is to allow the child to lead the parent in spontaneous play.**

Somehow as adults we have forgotten these marvelous lessons and have removed ourselves from spontaneous expression. I am reminded of the Yiddish humorist and novelist Leo Rosten. "You can understand and relate to most people better if you look at them—no matter how old or impressive they may be—as if they are children. For most of us never really grow up or mature all that much—we simply grow taller. Oh, to be sure, we laugh less and play less and wear uncomfortable disguises like adults, but beneath the costume is the child we always are, whose needs are simple, whose daily life is still best described by fairy tales."

Leading child psychologist Garry Landreth of the University of North Texas writes: "Our society may well be on the threshold of recognizing children as people, not as playthings, not as impersonal objects, not as sources of frustration to be tolerated until they mature, but as real people who possess unlimited potential and creative resources for growing, coping, and developing. Children are quite capable of teaching adults about themselves if adults are willing, patient, and open to learning."

A six-year-old child whose next-door neighbor had recently lost his wife went over to his neighbor's yard. Upon seeing the man sad, the little boy sat on his porch next to him. When his mother later learned where he was, she asked him what he had said to the neighbor. The little boy said, "Nothing, I just helped him cry."

Inviting the Parent to Play

Four-year-old Emily was tucking in her favorite doll for the night, when she asked her father to kiss her doll goodnight on the forehead. Three-year-old Alicia asked her mom to make room at the dinner table for her furry beanie rabbit. She told her mom that her rabbit was hungry, too. Without missing a beat, both parents showed their care and respect for their child's imaginary friend. These wise parents were modeling behavior on how to love and nurture outside of self. It was also an early sign of their accepting the tastes of and decisions made by their child. Always show respect for your child's relationship to her attachments. Parents who do not participate or take seriously such imaginative play will unwittingly undo a part of that special trust that a child wants to have with her parent.

To help us reconnect easier to our own childhood play and reinforce the child's self-expression, the parent should allow the child to decide who plays *what* character and with *what* toy. That means that the child gets to make up the rules and select whatever toy he wants to give you and to play with. If you're not sure what to do, just ask in a whisper voice, "Jonathan, what should I do with this?" I guarantee your child will tell you exactly what to do and where to do it. The focus for the parent should not be on the right way to use a toy, but the right process. The brilliant and pioneering work of child psychologists such as Virginia Axline, Haim Ginott, Garry Landreth, Clark Moustakas, Louise Guerney, and the late, wonderful television-visionary host and best friend Fred Rogers has taught us that play is where children learn meaning, spontaneity, and self-awareness. Spontaneous play provides a laboratory and proving ground for strategies to come to terms with the challenges of being, relating, and living. When a child plays, he is a manipulator; he makes do with whatever is at hand. His imagination transforms the commonplace into the priceless: a wooden block, rescued from under the living room couch and wrapped in a paper napkin, becomes a toy doll; a nickel thrust under a cushion becomes a buried treasure.

It is worth repeating and as a word of caution, a child's transitional object should never be used as a punishment or reward for behavior. For example, never say something like "David, if you keep pushing your brother, I'm going to take your little Woody friend away." At the same time, parents should not unnecessarily promote dependency past when the child has already relegated his little friend to the bottom of his chest of drawers. For example, if you see that your child is no longer asking or taking his cuddly friend to bed at night, it is best *not* to place it by your child's pillow just before he goes to bed. The same applies the following morning after you make his bed—do not put it on his pillow. This also includes not taking the transitional object as a backup soother for your child on car trips. Children are quite direct. If they want it, they will ask first.

It is worth repeating and as a word of caution, a child's transitional object should never be used as a punishment or reward for behavior.

Types of Play

In our fast-paced, fast-reacting world, it is easy to forget one of the most important activities of healthy child development: *free play*. Somehow, the marketing mavens on Wall Street have convinced millions of parents that buying smart toys and smart videos and overscheduling our children with rigid programs are good for them. Not so. Practically speaking, children engage in three primary categories of play. The first two kinds of play are common to all children, while the third kind of play is

reserved for children who may require professional intervention to work through severe problems or trauma.

1. **Play for fun:** This kind of play serves as the child's talk.
   The child is fully absorbed in play that usually transcends reality.
2. **Play for mastery:** Through manipulation and specific play
   objects, children engage in trial and error and repetitive
   play. This play is usually related to solving either a concrete
   problem or acting out others.
3. **Play to work through trauma:** This form of play is usually highlighted by complex behavioral problems revealing
   disturbing themes that require an outlet for catharsis and
   resolution. Children who have suffered specific trauma such
   as witnessing death, natural disasters, abuse, or their own
   parents' high-conflict marriage or divorce will do best under
   the care of an experienced play therapist.

A basic understanding of play will prove to be one of a parent's most important skills to draw on for many long years
to come. Imaginative play involves not only the enjoyment of
magic and symbols but also the ability for the child to distinguish between fantasy and reality. Some children want to dress
up for days or weeks in the same costume and may even want
to sleep in these costumes; such behavior may be seen as their
attempt to set the rules for their behavior and that of the characters they create. It may be time to eat dinner, but five-year-
old Rudy wants no part of that. "Spiderman doesn't eat real
food, he eats bugs," says Rudy to his father. His father, in an

effort to please (as opposed to guide), replies: "Yep. It's true, he eats bugs." Parents must always be careful not to overindulge their children in fantasy play and in doing so provide misguided reinforcement by letting their children believe, at one level or another, that they really do have superhuman powers. Six-year-old Steven, playing the role of Hulk, tells his mother, "Look at me—if I wanted, I could stop those trucks on the street." "Yes, you have those powers," his mother replies. A wiser response would be to redirect Steven to the reality of the situation yet at the same time acknowledge the fantasy. "Steven, it's fun to *pretend* you can stop those trucks. You're feeling strong. It's fun to pretend." By giving such a response, a parent would not interrupt the play or the child's feelings of having greater strength and power. When your child engages in fantasy play, expressions like "It's fun to pretend!" cannot be overused in reminding the child what is real and what is imaginary. This distinction is an important step to help prevent a potentially dangerous situation when you are not so close to protect.

Creativity of any kind incorporates free play, but it also must maintain a grip on the illusionary and the real. It is in this connection that the *transitional object* can have a vital role. The object is both real and illusionary to the child.

A Wireless Base

Ask any tech-savvy parent what a wireless base is and he will tell you it's his local Starbucks with a Wi-Fi connection. Unfortunately, this rousing trend is extending to our children

being plugged into a more dangerous base—the undoing of
the natural relationship between parent and child. No matter
how advanced today's toys and videos are, there can never be a
substitute for the good, old-fashioned, tethered, one-on-one
parent-child relationship.

> **No matter how advanced today's toys and videos are, there
> can never be a substitute for the good, old-fashioned, teth-
> ered, one-on-one parent-child relationship.**

Walk into virtually any super baby store and you will find a
huge selection of electric mobiles, battery-operated toy cell
phones, flashing plastic play stations that snap onto the front of
a stroller, and baby videotapes that teach music, mathematics,
science, and more. The problem with such items comes not
from their occasional use, but from their overuse as a substitute
relationship. One mother, who says she is not a morning person, puts on a series of educational videotapes for Jake, her
eighteen-month-old, every morning upon waking. For Jake,
his mornings include heavy doses of these so-called smart tapes
until his mom gains control of her mood. For similarly impatient parents, I have heard there is a new service on the Internet for $9.95 a month that offers a 24/7 Web page for your
baby to watch that changes every nine seconds. If you have any
doubt how popular this video fad is, more than $2 billion a
year is spent by parents who believe in these overhyped brain-
booster and educational toys for infants and toddlers. Most of
the reported studies hyping the increased IQ effect of listening

and watching these videos have, by and large, been debunked in professional journals.

Today's infants and young toddlers are getting plugged into these surrogate substitutes way too early. Today's infant toys look more like video game shows than the intended calming assortment of colors and shapes to manipulate. Meanwhile, our ubiquitous SUVs advertise built-in TV, DVD, and Internet access in the back of each seat to assist Mom and Dad in plugging their children into the granddaddy of all pacifiers: wireless games and entertainment. Each child has a different tolerance for such stimulation and isolation from family. Some children retreat and become withdrawn while others become overstimulated, resulting in increased moodiness and hyper behavior. I call this new trend "hooked on *sonics.*" When you reach chapter nine, look for the link between electronics and *hyperactivity.*

From Crib to Toddler Bed

As it is with stopping the pacifier and bottle habit, there is no "one time fits all" strategy for moving your child from his crib to a toddler bed. There is, however, an average age range of eighteen months to three years. This transition is clearly a milestone and will likely coincide with potty training and early preschool. I also recommend not starting potty training until he is out of the crib, so he is free to make it to the bathroom on his own. Otherwise it can be self-defeating.

As with all visible stages, both infantile and independent

behaviors can be seen in your child at the same time. Being aware of each type of behavior will help guide you in knowing when to make the switch. It is wise to wait until you see a consistent pattern of climbing out and staying out of the crib. Look for a strong will to do so. Often, toddlers attempt their escapes once in a while and are even successful from time to time. However, they also enjoy the safety and comfort of their own crib. Getting them a toddler bed too early can be frightening. You do not want to be ahead of your child's readiness, but rather in step with it. So don't panic and run out looking for that new decorator toddler bed *before* you see clear signs of independence. You can also extend the time your child stays in his crib by lowering the crib mattress as far down as possible so the side rails are higher and more difficult for him to climb over.

Part of first-time parents' contradictions in feelings during this stage is their concern for the safety of their toddler and the fun they will have in designing a whole new room around the new bed. Another reason parents become incentivized to make the early switch is that Mom is pregnant and about to give birth. Under these circumstances, I suggest that your toddler be given a two-month head start on getting used to his new digs before his new sister gets his old crib. Regardless of how well you prepare, odds are your toddler will show signs of regression with so much attention being focused on your newborn. He may even want to climb into his old crib again. By all means allow that behavior and remind him how special he was when he was a baby. "You're remembering what it felt like, aren't you? It felt good." Never degrade his desire to remember. You may even want to hold him (when you have the energy), singing the lullabies you used to sing to him. At the same time, do not feed too much into this behavior by serving him food in the crib or plugging in a TV! If you see your child is overextending himself in such fantasy, put some boundaries in place. "Barry, it's fun to pretend, but now it is time to return to your room and bed." These expressions will remind him of his new status as the older brother.

One final thought. When you do make the switch, try to place his bed in the same place the crib used to be, and by all means place all his transitional objects and blankets on his new bed! This is the most natural way to make the transition with the least amount of anxiety. Some parents purposely hide their child's favorite soft cuddlies, thinking such reminders will trigger infantile behavior. However, the opposite is true. If you do feel you have made the switch too soon, do your best not to go back unless you see that your child is panicked. Bringing back his crib after making such an important change will send the unmistakable signal that he is not getting bigger. It will also have a significant negative effect on his potty training. Do whatever you can within reason to resist his wanting to go back. This will pass, and you will have served your child well.

HERE ARE HOW SOME MOTHERS REMEMBER THEIR BOUTS WITH CRIB TRANSITIONS

So Adam is down for his afternoon nap, and I was browsing away on some catalog website, when all of a sudden, I hear this *bang* followed by *whaah!* I tear up to his room, fearing the worst, broken limbs, the works. He was shaking the crib so hard it knocked that thing over. I caught him with one leg hanging over. He's sixteen months now. Better start looking for a bed.

Out of three kids I had one climber. Once she figured out how to get out (she was fourteen months), that was it. Being that she was so little, I was afraid she'd get hurt falling or that some-how whatever she was wearing would get caught on the rail while she was jumping. I caught her a few times; she'd get on top of the rail and then hang by her fingers until she let go. Her other favorite thing was to stand on the dishwasher when the door was open and try to scramble up onto the counters. I think she is part monkey. I ended up getting her a full-size bed earlier than the other two.

I had two crib climbers, and I think it started when they were around eighteen months. My one son became very adept at climbing out so quietly that I wouldn't realize he was out until he came up on my bed to wake me up! The only warning sign I had with him was going into his bedroom, and upon seeing me, he would try to put his leg over the side. We did get him a toddler bed soon after that.

Sammy was twenty months and still happy staying in crib. We jump-started the process a little and took her crib mattress and put it on the floor at the side of her bed, and if she did fall out, it was onto the mattress.

My oldest son (or should I say monkey) climbed out of his crib at twelve months. Yep. I put him down for a nap, went downstairs, and not five minutes later heard this big *thud* followed by footsteps. I met him at his bedroom doorway. He smiled at me and said, "Mama!" We went out the next day and bought a toddler bed. I actually hid in his closet to see how he was getting out. He'd turn his feet inward and basically climb the slats. Funny thing was, we got him a toddler daybed and turned it so the only open side was against the wall, and he couldn't figure out how to get out of it for about a month. The child could scale the slats of his crib, but couldn't get over an eight-inch side of a toddler bed!

THREE

Regressive Behavior

The next time you talk to a little child, look deeply into his eyes. Don't just glance at him, or over him, or through him. Look straight through those wide-open, unguarded "eye portals" into his mind. You'll feel an answering, almost forgotten stirring in your mind. You'll be in touch with innocence and the long-ago. Do it— for it's one of the best things in life!

—ART LINKLETTER

Three Steps Forward, One Step Back

Norman was doing just fine. Third grade was going well; his ninth birthday was only three weeks away. One night he was frantically going through his closet. "Finally, I found it," he said. It was his old pal Ralphie, his favorite puppet lion when he was five.

It seems as though it comes from nowhere! Your child was showing all the signs of breakthrough maturity, and then regression rears it head. Seven-year-old Robert all of a sudden is afraid of the dark. Carolyn, age five, is asking her mom for her old baby blanket. Five-year-old Alex has been climbing into his sister's crib when she's not there—pretending to be a baby again. Such regressive behavior can make any parent feel anxious and perplexed.

It's no secret we live in a world where quick answers have a greater premium than an understanding of *why* certain behaviors come to be in the first place. This insatiable need for a quick fix should be tempered by first asking *why?* Such understanding can at the very least help prevent a few disruptive weeks or months from becoming a serious stage or pattern. Without an understanding of why certain behaviors occur, it becomes almost impossible to gain real insight. Though the disturbing behavior in question may abate for a while, it will likely reappear later in some other form of combative and non-compliant behavior. Under certain circumstances, where the parent-child relationship is weak, a child may become more dependent on his transitional object for comfort than he is on his parents. "Little Otis," a small, soft teddy bear, will never reject Nathan when he feels scared. It is my hope that armed with this new understanding, you will both react and be available in a different way should your child begin to show signs of regressive behavior.

The following are a few regressive behaviors that children may engage in when parts of their lives become *too* stressful, along with some suggested remedies.

SEPARATION ANXIETY

Any early stage of development that involves separation and independence from a parent(s) may cause a youngster to feel insecure. At two, for instance, toddlers often become apprehensive about being alone and playing alone. When they enter preschool, fearfulness may make an encore appearance. Many working parents also report that after they return to work, their young toddlers become unbelievably clingy, crying so hard that upon their return the children don't want them out of sight even at home. By the time a child is ready to leave home for preschool at around the age of four or so, he should be able to follow someone else's direction, be respectful, responsible, and fun to be around. During those first four years of life, a child learns from his parents that the world is a safe and caring place. The quality of the bonding during this critical period reinforces the kind of loving relationship with the parents, which directly determines many of the thresholds for frustration and tolerance. Generally, the first representative of our society who recognizes that there may be social and behavioral problems is the kindertarten teacher.

Fortunately, there are some things you can do to create a more secure feeling in your child and to make these times apart more comfortable. If your child normally cries when you go to work, for instance, don't complicate the situation by sneaking out the back door when the babysitter arrives. An important first step is to carefully talk about leaving before it happens. This needs to occur in a calm way day after day, even as your child is crying. "I know you wish I would stay all day and play with you, but it is time for me to go to work now. I'll be back by four o'clock." You can talk about where you are going and why, and when you will get back. Even if your child doesn't understand everything you are saying, this kind of talk is reassuring. When you sneak out and disappear, it confuses a child and reminds him of his worst nightmare, abandonment. Social worker Deborah Hage points out that while on the one hand a child is made furiously angry by a parent's threat to desert, on the other hand, he dare not express that anger in case it makes the parent actually do so. This is the main reason why in these cases anger at a parent usually turns repressed and is then redirected to other targets—adults, siblings, children, friends—or even more vulnerable targets—feeble schoolmates, and so on.

To counter such a reaction, be direct; try to slow down your morning departure. Be sure you look relaxed and reflect back your child's anxiousness. "I can see you don't want me to leave." "I will be back in seven hours." It is important to keep reflecting back and ending with a time when you will return. Prepare your child in the same way for babysitters, and don't make a big deal about saying good-bye. It helps to hand her security blanket or doll to her, if she has one. It would also be helpful if you could ask your babysitter to occasionally talk to your child about where you are and what you are doing. She can say something like, "Mommy's at work, but she's coming back in the afternoon." It can also help if you leave some pictures of yourself around where your child can see them and reach them. Encourage the babysitter to talk about them and let your child pick them up when she wants to.

For toddlers who really struggle with separation, practice saying good-bye and hello when you are home—such as when you go from one room to another. For example, when you are about to leave a room say, "I'm going upstairs to change," and then upon returning, make a game of it by smiling and saying, "Hello, I'm back!" Your reassuring smile and fun attitude will reinforce his feelings of security.

Old patterns of clinginess and regression are almost always linked to some event. They can stem from something as simple as the normal resistance a child experiences as he moves from one psychosocial stage to another, or, in more complex cases, they can be initiated by a stressful school environment, the birth of a new sibling, trauma, marital conflict, or divorce. They can also be brought on by a simple but abrupt shift in routine—such as switching carpools or changing babysitters. An old or new transitional object close at hand makes whatever is bothering that child a bit more tolerable. Children are usually very good at dealing with minor changes, but some feel very threatened if they haven't been adequately prepared first. These children require heaps of reassurance. Unfortunately, parents can unwittingly extend certain unwanted behaviors in their children that they wish to extinguish by being impatient.

Equally important to overcoming clinginess is a child's ability to learn how to play independently. To teach a toddler to be with himself, give him an occasional soft touch on the shoulder as he plays and then keep walking. Do not talk or pick him up. If you provide him with a brief soft touch or smile, you'll be giving him reassurance without interrupting what he's doing. If the child is older—say, three or four—sit down and play alongside him; as he becomes engrossed in the activity, quietly get up and walk away for about thirty seconds. Over the next few days, lengthen the absence by a few minutes. Parents should continue to give soft touches now and then to remind him that they are close by. Even school-age children can be trained to play alone if parents take the time to start a suitable project—such as constructing a model or molding designs with clay. Expressions such as "You know how to do that" or "Play the way you want" will help the child focus on himself; then gradually you can withdraw from the area. Be sure to return after about five minutes and recognize your child's effort. Do not use over-the-top, phony praise about how fantastic or beautiful his work is. Rather, "Wow, Emily, look what you made."

It's important to let a clingy child experience longer separations as well. Parents should also make a point of hiring a babysitter from time to time so that they can go out for an entire evening: it's good for the child and good for the marriage. If you can't bring yourself to part with your child for even a few hours, the message you'll send to her is that she is not safe with anyone else but you. As the moment of departure draws near, a child may become agitated, but parents should remain firm and supportive. Offer her a favorite teddy bear as a companion, or promise to call her at home later. Then leave right away—protracting the good-bye scene will only make the separation more painful for everyone.

As a rule, I advise parents to prepare their toddlers for these separations by talking about them ahead of time. If you are going to the supermarket or to work and must leave your child with a sitter or friend, give your child some detail so he can visualize what you will be doing. For example: "Jonathan, in fifteen minutes I am going to the supermarket to buy some cantaloupe, oranges, and chicken. I will be picking out the fruit in the produce section. Later, we will eat it together. I will be back in one hour. I know you understand." This may seem like too much information for a twenty-month-old toddler, but you will find that this kind of detail and *talking up* both reduces anxiety and helps your child visualize you while you are gone. When you return home, make sure you remind him of what you said earlier. "You waited well, Jonathan. I was back in fifteen minutes just like I said. You did it!" Keep in mind, though, that making too big a deal about a future separation in advance will make an already anxious child even more worried. Don't make a moment into an event. Be confident and steadfast in your casual manner.

With little or no intervention from Mom and Dad, most kids overcome their clinginess. That means not overreacting to a child's fears with smothering hugs and words of sympathy, but instead, if he seems fearful or tense, simply tell him calmly, "I know this is difficult for you, but you can do it." If a child's clinginess is a reaction to a major change in the family, such as death or divorce, try to help him express what's troubling him. Sometimes it's useful to read to a child—especially storybooks about these difficult experiences. Address the situation, read about it, lay out the problem with dolls or puppets, even draw pictures with him. Gradually, your child should begin to feel that he has some control over the situation. In extremely rare cases, a child's reluctance to stray from his parent's side may be a sign of a more serious psychological problem. If a youngster refuses to go to school or leave the house, or if he experiences full-blown panic attacks, mothers and fathers should consult a play therapist to work through the source of his fears. But remember that for the vast majority of kids, clinginess is perfectly normal and temporary, so don't rush to a therapist just because a three-year-old fusses about being left with a babysitter. Chances are that with a little effort, parent and child will be able to resolve the problem.

Here are some reported common situations and solutions involving separation with infants and toddlers.

Although four-year-old Becky is terrified of starting pre-school, her new teacher seems friendly and sympathetic. This morning, she threw a temper tantrum in the parking lot and Mom had to carry her into the building. Solution: it is best to talk to your child in advance about what she can expect from her new classroom routine. Waiting till the last minute will only increase anxiety. Reassure her that you'll return to pick her up in a few hours. If her teacher permits, stay with her for the first ten minutes as she adjusts to her new class. It may also help to have the teacher match her with a friendly buddy who can show her around and play with her. This new playmate will invariably introduce her to other kids, and in time your child will feel less overwhelmed.

You're visiting a friend who has an infant close in age to your ten-month-old son. Her baby is playing quietly with her toys on a blanket on the floor, but every time you try to put your child down next to her, he cries loudly and wants to be picked up. It seems as if he won't spend a minute with anyone but you. Solution: it's not unusual for a child of this age to demonstrate such clingy behavior. Sit down on the blanket with him on your lap and begin to play with the toys and the other baby. As your child begins to feel more secure, remove him from your lap and gradually withdraw to a chair where he can see you. If the visit works out, repeat it soon to rein-force your baby's behavior. Eventually, you may be able to leave the room for short periods, as long as another adult is present.

Recently, your seven-year-old has strongly resisted going to bed at night. Every evening, he requests a drink of water, an extra blanket, a story, and when you try to leave the room, he bursts into tears. Solution: begin by attempting to find out what's bothering your child. Try telling a made-up story together, setting up a situation similar to your child's and asking him to help you develop a storyline. His responses may provide a clue to his anxieties. Another solution: Several hours before bedtime, have a discussion about the nighttime rules: Once a story is read and the lights are out, you'll sit in his room for a while until he feels safe, but he must rest quietly in bed. If he breaks the rules, leave the room for twenty seconds or so. Be sure to acknowledge how well he handled the twenty seconds alone. Say it in a calm, serious tone—one of respect. "Douglas, you really handled that well." When you reenter, explain again that you'll remain in the room only if he tries to fall asleep. In this way, you'll be providing support without encouraging the sort of elaborate bedtime rituals that many children rely on.

OVEREATING

As a child reaches five years of age, food can become an unsuspected transitional addiction. We see this pattern of overeating increasing in our children across the United States. According to a 2003 Centers for Disease Control and Prevention report, one in three American children born in 2000 will become diabetic later in life unless they start eating less and exercising more. Aware of these dangerous patterns, food manufacturers continue to create and market their juices and sugary, fatty snack foods with messages to both children and parents that they are "fun and good for you." Emotional overeating is no longer reserved as a delicious transitional object just for adults. Now six-year-old Dana, while watching television or playing on the computer, can munch and crunch for hours on end. Overall, 39 percent of the girls who now are healthy three-year-olds and 33 percent of boys of the same age are likely to develop diabetes in their lives. These are startling statistics! Authorities believe that nearly 6 percent of the American population already has diabetes. Globally, the World Health Organization has estimated that by 2025, the number of people with diabetes worldwide will more than double, from 140 million to 300 million. Most of these potential cases can be prevented. If you see your child withdrawing from his world and reaching for snack food *before* reaching for his sneakers, get involved and get him active!

According to a 2003 Centers for Disease Control and Prevention report, one in three American children born in 2000 will become diabetic later in life, unless they start eating less and exercising more.

HEAD-BANGING

Watching a toddler engage in head-banging for the first time can be pretty scary. When in distress, some children may attempt to soothe themselves by repetitively banging their head against a mattress or headboard, rolling their head, or rocking the bed. The behavior can appear violent and can be caused by any number of changes, including family conflict or the *premature* removal of a pacifier or a favorite blanket. Head-banging, however, is not the kind of self-soothing that calms a child down in the way that pacifiers, thumb-sucking, or holding a favorite object does. It is, after all, a kind of attack on himself and it closes the child off from the reassurance and help he really needs. By firmly intervening and holding the child during these times, you may significantly limit or stop the behavior and give your child the feeling, comfort, and secure base that he needs. To help discharge the child's excess energy and tension, hobbyhorse rockers and swings can lessen such patterns. In the evening, at bedtime, keep all activity quiet and calm, including any marital discord.

KIDS MAY HOP IN YOUR BED

If you share your bed with your children, you are not alone. Surveys show that 25 to 30 percent of American parents routinely let their children sleep with them, either for part or all of the night. The problem, however, is for those children who have been successfully sleeping by themselves in their own bed and now want to return to the parents' bed. Naturally, this new behavior can be the result of any number of reasons. With the obvious exception of a traumatic event, it is best for the parent to remain consistent in returning the child to his own bed. In terms of sequencing, an initial talk should take place the following day, preferably after school, with the explanation, "David, remember last night how you wanted to climb into our bed? [Wait for response.] Well, from tonight and here on, everyone will sleep in his own bed. Your brother will stay in his bed, you will stay in your bed, and Mom and Dad will stay in their bed. If there is something important you need, you can come and see me." Include such reassurances as "I know you can do this. Let me know you understand." [Wait for response.] About an hour and a half before bedtime, an additional reminder about what you talked about earlier should be issued, as this will give the child time to prepare. Keep your reminder short, no more than thirty seconds, and say it in a firm and matter-of-fact way without anger, so as not to set in motion a contest. If your child does come in your bed in the middle of the night, and in all likelihood he will again, be sure to walk or carry him directly back to his bed, with no conversation until you get there. Then repeat the rule you stated earlier. As he continues to cry and whine to stay with you, you simply keep repeating the rule. Be firm and confident, and leave. If the child continues to cry, you must do your best to ignore it. If he returns to your room, repeat the sequence again and again. With each interval of his returning to your bed, spend no more than thirty seconds returning him to his bed. Initially, a child can test you up to twenty-five times a night. While this simplistic and repetitive approach can seem monotonous and exhausting for the parent, it *will* work. Parents often become more bored than the child does hearing the same words repeated over and over.

In cases involving high-conflict divorce, or in marriages where high conflict is the order of the day, both child and parent may get used to sleeping in the same bed.

In cases involving high-conflict divorce, or in marriages where high conflict is the order of the day, both child and parent may get used to sleeping in the same bed. Each may find sharing a bed a way to assuage feelings of aloneness and insecurity. Such a pattern can easily become an unhealthy transitional ritual, and in almost all cases the child welcomes such attention; however, if there is a constancy of cuddling and closeness as parent and child fall asleep together, then these actions will interfere with a child's sense of autonomy. Personal boundaries can be violated and confusing for the child, and the ritual is a false and misleading oedipal symbol of winning over the mother or father. Depending upon his age, this is complicated by the latent sexual undertones of such interaction felt by the child. What may appear to a parent as simple hugging affection stimulates confusion in the child and brings up more questions and conflict than a parent may realize. There is a vast difference between having an infant or two-year-old sleeping in the parents' bed, and the ritual of a child five, seven, or nine years old diving under the covers at night and wrapping herself around Dad, or Mom wrapping herself around her son and falling asleep in that position. Such rituals reinforce an unhealthy attachment to sleeping with a parent, in contrast to a healthy attachment to a blanket or stuffed animal. Complicating it further, a parent's habit in sleepwear— full pajamas, half pajamas, no pajamas, underwear, and so on— may violate healthy, personal boundaries. For all of these reasons, intimate cuddling must be examined and at the very least stopped.

BED-WETTING

One of the most common causes of bed-wetting (enuresis) is stress and trauma; divorce and marital conflict are also major factors in the occurrence, reemergence, or increased frequency of bed-wetting episodes. Younger children are more likely to experience this, but older children—as old as nine to fourteen—can find themselves bed-wetting again. It is fairly common for children with no history of wetting the bed to experience this as a result of stress from problems such as school-related problems or fear.

In high-conflict marriages or divorce, putting a child in a position to choose loyalty is always damaging and confusing. Regardless of fault, a child needs to think of both parents as competent. Gestures, comments, or statements aimed at degrading a spouse will cause an increase in a child's stress and may ultimately be manifested in bed-wetting. Regardless of what one parent thinks about or feels for the other, the child must never be put in a position to choose loyalties. With the U.S. Department of Vital Statistics pegging the current divorce rate at 52.4 percent, a child's immediate concern is how divorce and continuous marital conflict will affect his daily life, including wondering about keeping his room.

So how should a parent react to a child's bed-wetting? Empathy and preserving a child's self-respect are crucial. Let the child know that you understand that he is upset and that this is temporary. Reassure him that with practice, he will overcome this hurdle. Offer to assist: after the bed is wet say, "Okay, you pull off the sheets and I'll get a fresh set." It is fine if the child prefers to make the bed alone—he may be embarrassed. Making the bed should not be viewed as a punishment. The tone should not be scolding. Having to make a bed will not motivate a child to overcome bed-wetting. The child's most significant fear is that his parents may be angry or, at the very least, disappointed. Most children are aware that their "accidents" cause smells that are considered unacceptable, as well as unwanted increased laundry. But remember, as with any real solution, the resolution of bed-wetting will take time. It's a poor idea to put a time frame on the process or to go overboard with praise if the child has been successful for a week. Chances are good that he will slip back for a time. Misplaced praise at the wrong time will pressure and frustrate the child.

Encouragement vs. Praise

As a child continues to strive to do what is before him, parents must convey two critical child-guidance principles: faith in the child's ability and encouragement in recognition of effort. Clark Moustakis, the renowned child psychologist, expressed it best. "Most importantly, there is *faith*. Not so much in the process (that is a given) but in the child! There is no clear-cut formula by which a parent conveys faith in a child. Faith is an intangible quality perceived largely through the presence of feelings, body language, and expressions. It is unspoken as much as it is spoken. It generates energy and inspiration and creates a feeling of well-being. When someone has faith in us, we are encouraged to face ourselves and express ourselves as the person we really are."

Encouragement is a much stronger incentive than praise: praise focuses on the end result, but encouragement focuses entirely on the effort.

Along with faith, a second critical child guidance principle is to *encourage*. Encouragement is a much stronger incentive than praise: praise focuses on the end result, but encouragement focuses entirely on the effort. More specifically, it is the *full* effort a child or adult makes in an attempt to do something that measures true success! An honest effort must always be rewarded with respect. It is the secret elixir leading to solid performance. Consider, for example, a third-grader who has fallen behind in his schoolwork and works all weekend to catch up: the teacher who on Monday morning tells the boy that it's too late misses a critical opportunity to connect with the child and reinforce the importance of his remarkable effort. A wise teacher would reward such effort with an A+. Years from now, the workbook will long be forgotten, but not the memory of that successful effort.

In encouraging effort, the parent or teacher should eliminate the word *try* from all communication. It has a weak and wimpy meaning, implying a quick-and-quit context. "Well, Mommy, I tried, but I can't." The next time you ask your child to try something that may be difficult for him, substitute the word *effort* where you would normally say *try*. "You know, Zack, I know you are going to give your full effort to breaking your thumb-sucking habit. I know you understand what that means." Even a four-year-old can sense the power behind the words *full effort*.

A parent who praises a child for completing a task or behaving correctly—"I'm so proud of you for carrying your plate to the sink"; "I'm so proud of you when you share with your brother"—will likely make the child feel that her parent is proud *only* when certain tasks or behaviors are completed correctly. Such praise unfortunately leaves no room to recognize the real prize—*the effort*. In the case of the child carrying the plate, she will often hand it to the parent first. The effort to have picked up the plate in the first place is what must be recognized. Pressure can also be an inevitable side effect of this praise. A child who is successful at something by just getting lucky may quit the activity prematurely because of the pressure to duplicate the accomplishment again and possibly fail. Praise has two parts: the first part is what we tell the child; the second and more important part is *what the child tells himself!*

Praise has two parts: the first part is what we tell the child; the second and more important part is *what the child tells himself!*

No single influence on this subject has been greater than that of legendary UCLA coach John Wooden. Recently honored at the White House at age ninety-three, he has taught generations about the real secrets of bringing up children and what it takes to be a winning human being. It might seem odd to invoke the name of John Wooden in a book about young children and transitional objects, but if you were to read his autobiography or read about his work on the Web, you would understand completely. His relationships and work with young athletes personified the transitional change. His legendary pyramid of success was based on effort and faith, *not* praise.

If we look more closely at the real effects of praise, we'll find that *evaluative praise* can backfire, having a negative effect on a child's feelings about himself. When a parent praises a child as a good boy or good girl for helping around the house, the child may be left to wonder whether he or she is a bad boy or bad girl when not helping. In contrast, encouragement lets a child know that you believe in her ability. Encouragement recognizes any effort, even if the end result is not achieved. Encouragement feels like permission. If, for instance, a parent sees a child at the playground walking over to a piece of equipment he has not used, and upon arrival the child is very tentative, the parent might say, "You're thinking of climbing those"—which lets the child know it is okay, yet still empowers the child to make the final decision. Effective encouraging expressions leave the child with an opportunity to praise himself. It is more important in the long run for the child to believe she can do something than for the parent to just say so.

Children are perceptive and often more critical of themselves than we realize. They sometimes will not accept real praise; most will see through phony praise quickly. A good ratio is 75 percent encouragement to 25 percent praise. Some children who are constantly praised become addicted to such recognition and learn the likes and the dislikes of the parent, adult, or teacher praising them in order to ensure a steady stream of praise. It is as though adult recognition becomes more important than their own likings. The child who, when playing with a parent, *repeatedly* asks the parent to choose the activity may be one for whom pleasing others may be overly important. An insightful parent who wants to help the child be more comfortable in her own choices might say, "You want to make sure that you do what I like. When we play your games, you decide what we should do." If these responses sound therapeutic, they are. They are proven communication techniques that will help children develop and find their authentic self. Here are some encouraging expressions that will help your child believe in himself more:

You can do it.

You can decide how to do that.

Wow. You did that. You're excited about the way you got that to work.

You thought you couldn't do that, but you made a full effort anyway.

You're working hard on that. No matter how hard it is, you keep at it!

You are very important.

Great discovery.

Nothing can stop you now.

You're catching on now.

Bravo!

You're on target.

You remembered what you needed to know.

You reminded yourself.
You must have been practicing.

Eight Ways to Help Your Toddler Feel Bigger!

How we make our child feel about his transitional object can also have a direct impact on the child's sense of social self-confidence. No parent wants to watch her two- or four-year-old start to cry just because a playmate grabbed her special teddy bear or because she tripped and fell down suddenly. Likewise, no parent wants to watch his child be bullied or remain timid in the face of everyday challenges and confrontations. There are ways to help your child strengthen her determination, tolerance, and competence *faster*. Naturally, some children have a greater potential for solving their social frustrations than others—their temperament is their natural control lever. However, a parent who can successfully guide and create more opportunities for his child to feel successful will reinforce the child's inner feelings that "Hey, I can really do it!"

A parent who can successfully guide and create more opportunities for his child to feel successful will reinforce the child's inner feelings that "Hey, I can really do it!"

As the child grows from total dependence to mature dependence, early transitional objects are sometimes left behind and replaced by new behaviors. At this point, the relationship with the mother or the transitional object may have been subsumed in the wider social influences process, with the child now being able to participate *more* spontaneously in what comes his way.

To encourage such behavior, here are some ideas to help accelerate maturity when certain behaviors seem stuck.

WHEN YOUR TODDLER FALLS, DON'T ACT LIKE IT'S FUN BY SAYING SILLY THINGS LIKE "OOPS" OR "BOOM"

Falling is our body's natural way of teaching balance as well as consequences. Although it often brings more surprise than pain, we don't want to mask its meaning. Falling is not fun and it can hurt. It takes concentration to learn not to do it. Acting like it is fun is really making fun of children when they are trying so hard not to fall and yet still do. This, of course, is different from showing enthusiasm and having fun in helping them walk: I am addressing only when they fall! If you think this kind of thinking is over the top or is taking two-year-olds' feelings too seriously, then you are grossly underestimating the enormous range of a young child's ability to understand. A young toddler or even five-year-old will read an adult's face for cues about herself. If your face is cringing from the fall or disapproving from saying "oops" or looking happy after saying "boom," your message may be different than how your child feels and can be confusing to her. Sometimes as parents we want to take the pain away, and this is what we need to watch out for in ourselves. When your children fall, let them see you watch with confidence by saying, "Yes, Deanna, I saw!" When they stand, be there to recognize their achievement with, "Yes, Deanna, I see you got up!" Think of yourself learning to ski—you fall and someone says "boom"?

DON'T ALWAYS RUN WHEN YOUR CHILD FALLS

Unless it is very serious, wait a few moments before aiding your child when she falls. This hesitation allows her to decide on her own, without your visual cue, whether or not something is wrong and she needs help. Just those few moments of hesitation, along with a neutral expression, can change feelings of helplessness and dependence to self-sufficiency. If, for example, we ask too soon, "Is everything okay?" we encourage the child to think, "Maybe I'm *not* okay . . . I thought I was! I better take the help." If you think this example is an over-dramatization, think again. Parents who *continuously* express their love and concern this way are missing an important opportunity for their child to get in touch with her own self-reliance. Later, that child turned adult may find herself seeking doctors and medicine prematurely for routine matters she could easily treat herself.

DON'T OFFER A BAND-AID OR CANDY MEDICINE SO FAST

Often, beginning very early in life, an overprotective parent or caretaker will overreact when a child falls or appears to have hurt himself, jumping to the rescue even before the child provides the cue whether the matter is serious or not. "Let's put some medicine on this," a parent may say *too* quickly, or "Let's put a Band-Aid on that and it will feel better." From this, the child learns that he will feel better by taking something and can get extra attention by extending his crying. A better way (assuming that the matter is not serious) is to say empathetically, "Tommy, that could hurt" or "Show me where it happened." Children prefer to hear that you recognize how much something hurt more than they want the remedy. However, if you reinforce the "poor little you" attitude, then the attention and helpless feelings will continue to prosper. Some children deliberately put themselves in more perilous situations or even the slightest discomfort to get the parent or caretaker to listen to their complaining, so they can be held or soothed. I'm not suggesting that we treat the child in a detached way; I am saying we must let the child send us the signal *first*. Too many times a parent will send the cue *something is wrong* before it actually is! Just as we shouldn't reach for an aspirin too fast, we must not reach too fast to solve our children's problems.

STOP CALLING YOUR CHILD PET NAMES

Your child's name is far more pleasing for him to hear than any pet name. More important, by using it you will encourage more mature behavior than you will by calling out "Sweet Pea" or "Little Monkey." Pet names or nicknames like Mikey for Michael or Ben-E-Boo for Ben are in direct conflict with a child's natural development and desire to be big. This is not to suggest that parents who call their children by nicknames are doing psychological damage. However, if the intent is to strengthen identity and advance maturity, then calling your child by his real name will help do just that. In addition, pet names can be derogatory and may unwittingly encourage your child to act out more. For example, a child who is often called "my little monster" will over time likely assume some of that behavior. In other situations, when your child is acting silly, don't call him silly. Name calling or for that matter comparing your child's behavior to that of someone else you regard as more appropriate will encourage more resistance and *more* silliness. It is better to focus on and recognize desirable behavior by saying words like "Bobby, I see you don't really want to talk now." This will help your child gain control faster and send the signal he can do it.

IF YOUR CHILD HAS TO GO TO THE BATHROOM, SOMETIMES MAKE HIM WAIT

Nature's call provides a great opportunity to help your child feel good about his ability to control himself physically. (Obviously, if he is in the middle of potty training, this is not advisable.) This waiting method is recommended for four- and five-year-olds, and it will take a little judgment (and guts) on your part to recognize when they can *really* hold it in long enough to get home or wherever you are going. However, in the end, exercising such self-control will be a kind of milestone for your child. Later, in a real situation where you *truly cannot* find a bathroom, you can remind your child of the time he held it in. The ability to use mind over physical discomfort will be an important theme for him growing up and another lesson in self-reliance.

LEARN TO EXCHANGE HAND SIGNALS LIKE THE THUMBS-UP SIGNAL

Less talk, no talk: exchanging few or no words can be quite effective in building children's confidence. Try the thumbs-up signal when they recover from a fall or tummy ache or even when you're walking away after dropping them off at school. It signals your confidence in them and puts the focus on their self-reliance.

WHEN YOUR CHILD GETS HURT, SHOW HIM WHERE IT HAPPENED

Except when immediate first aid is necessary, return to the exact place of the accident. Curiosity about where the accident happened will provide the child with more comfort than any lecture: "Stevie, it happened right here on the edge of the door." Children always want to know the *how* of everything; watch your child's face change to a more calm expression when you point out and replay the events. When you are finished showing and explaining, he may continue crying, but don't take that as an indication that your tactic didn't work. The child just wants reassurance. Repeating words like "That can hurt" to validate his experience is better than saying "There, there, that's not so bad" or "I'll bet you'll never do that again." Children, like adults, want to feel you have empathy for how they feel—rather than have you convey an attitude of feeling sorry for them. The ability to replay the injury or trauma shows the child that he can face it and gives him time to work out a different ending in his own mind. "Hey, I handled that okay."

HELP A CHILD STAND UP FOR HIMSELF AROUND OBNOXIOUS OR CONTROLLING PEOPLE

One way to help make a child feel more self-confident and less *invisible* when confronted by a controlling adult or child is to help her express the right response. For some withdrawn children, these moments can be frequent. It doesn't matter whether the person in question is a visiting grandmother, a total stranger, or a more aggressive child at the park—having nothing to say will make a child feel weak and small. If we can show her how to speak up, and model this kind of behavior, she can begin to see herself emerging victorious. For example, a good time to advocate for your child may arise when Aunt Carole says, "You can't leave without a kiss," or an uncle says, "Are you going to act shy now?" Words like "Looks like you don't want to kiss Aunt Carole now, maybe later" or "Michelle isn't being shy, she's just not in the mood now, maybe another time" work to take pressure off the child and give guidance on how she might handle similar situations in the future. Don't worry about the adults' feelings. Your first priority is your child's well-being. When you give these responses, look at your child's face. Chances are good that you will see an expression that says, "Boy, it feels good when Mommy understands me." Later, this kind of mutual communication will translate to a more cooperative and self-reliant child who will handle new situations with greater ease—it both teaches her how and gives her permission to speak up!

FOUR

How to Set Limits

Being supportive often means waiting and listening, and
more waiting, until you're better able to understand the
drama that a certain child is living through
at the moment.

—FRED ROGERS

Setting Limits

All parents agree that children need limits. What they don't agree on are the methods and the timing for setting them. They live with their children from moment to moment, exacting obedience or excusing disobedience on whim rather than on principle. The solution to this predicament, however, may lie in the approach. Some parents think that setting limits is a one-time event. It shouldn't be. It is a dynamic process that keeps changing. A two- or three-year-old, although still several years away from far greater limit-setting rules, can begin to process what you mean when you say, "Ellen, remember what I said about two more pieces of candy. You've had those two, we're all done now!"

Young children respond better to limits when parents are specific rather than general about what they *will* or *will not* allow. For example, if a parent says, "Darren, you can only have the bottle for a *little while* longer," Darren will not understand this vague limit. Does "little" mean one hour or a half hour? He will make sure to find out! Better to be specific and tell Darren, as you point to your watch, he has three more minutes to keep his bottle. Although he will still complain when the time comes to put down his bottle, he will be prepared to understand time better, and he will *not* be as confused when the time comes to enforce it. Be specific: "Sarah, it's time to leave in five minutes" rather than "Soon it will be time to leave."

Sometimes parents will prepare a child to believe that they mean business by faking a stern look, threatening a consequence, or lowering their voice with seriousness. They believe this will have a greater impact on their child. It doesn't. Children can read and gauge how authentic and committed parents are in enforcing what they say. However, when used correctly, voice and facial expressions become the *real* tools for keeping potential problems from escalating.

When used correctly, voice and facial expressions become the *real* tools for keeping potential problems from escalating.

Parental consistency in setting and enforcing limits will determine how easily new limits will be accepted by the child. As a rule, limits should be set in relation to what is *truly* important to you and your child. They should be enforced consistently, with a consequence *every single time* they are broken. This is key if a child is to really believe you mean what you say and you say what you mean.

SETTING LIMITS MAKES A CHILD FEEL SAFE

In addition to the greater child compliance that results from maintaining reasonable limits, setting limits also allows a child to *feel* safe and *be* safe. Enforcement of your established limit helps the child to be less anxious and less empowered. Conversely, unenforced limits will cause increased anxiety in your child's everyday life with you as a result of his not knowing when or how your hammer of discipline will fall. The child will know when he has broken a rule and will become anxious about when the punishment or retaliation will occur. He will also become more noncompliant in an environment where limits are inconsistently enforced. Parents who are not skillful in maintaining limits bestow a false authority to the child, which leads the child to think he's smarter and tougher than his parents. It is confirmation for him that he has defeated an adult. Yet although he celebrates his victory, he is also scared and uncertain of his new power: Who will keep him safe? Who will protect him? In addition to inconsistent or no enforcement of rules, other ineffective methods from a child's point of view are lectures and long explanations. Both signal a weakness in a parent's willpower to follow through with consequences. Children interpret these long talks as "My parents prefer to talk rather than act."

Ineffective methods from a child's point of view are lectures and long explanations. Both signal a weakness in a parent's willpower to follow through with consequences. Children interpret these long talks as "My parents prefer to talk rather than act."

Consequences

There are three basic consequences that can occur when a child does not abide by an established rule: natural consequences, logical consequences, and unrelated consequences.

NATURAL CONSEQUENCES

Natural consequences follow as direct results of a behavior; they are an outcome, or consequence, that you don't have to impose. For example, a child who doesn't come to the table on time will find his food cold!

LOGICAL CONSEQUENCES

Logical consequences are ones you must impose upon a child but which have a direct connection with the broken limit. For example, if a child is playing a game on your computer and leaves your computer screen with confusing icons, he loses his computer privileges for several days. Same for a bicycle: it is much easier for a child to make the connection between leaving the bike outside and not being allowed to ride it the following day than it would be for her to make the connection between leaving the bike outside and an unrelated consequence like not watching television or being allowed to go to a friend's house.

UNRELATED CONSEQUENCES

Unrelated consequences are those that you impose as a last re-
sort when natural or logical consequences haven't worked.
Even when using unrelated consequences, however, never go
overboard with severe punishment. Remember the goal: you
are trying to teach the child to master behavior on his own.
Severe punishment defeats a child's learning. A child is likely
to remember the extreme punishment and forget the rule he
broke. Later, when you are *not* around, he will likely repeat the
transgression. An example of an unrelated consequence would
be punishing a child by not taking him to get a pair of sneakers you promised him because he was mean to his brother.

THINK TWICE BEFORE SETTING A LIMIT OR RULE

Any parent who seeks to make rules and set limits must first
answer the question: "Am I prepared to enforce them?" This
holds true for the long term as well as the short term. If you
are at the beach, for instance, and your child keeps whining for
something she wants, and you threaten her with leaving, are
you prepared to quietly pack up your child, blanket, umbrella,
chair, cooler and leave? If the answer is no, do not set that limit.
As a rule, ask yourself, "Is this limit necessary? Does it fit the
situation? Will I enforce it?" A limit or a rule that is heavy-
handed and unfair is sometimes worse than no limit at all.
For example, five-year-old Carol was touching the packages
of candy while waiting in line at the supermarket with her
mother. "Carol, *no!* Remember the rule about no touching in

the store. When we get home, you will stay in your room for one hour."

Naturally, parents must set reasonable, specific rules and enforce them. One afternoon, three-and-a-half-year-old Alex was riding in the car with his mother on their way to run some errands. She told him, "Alex, I'm warning you, if you don't behave, I'm going to take you home." This simple statement had three problems with it. First, the mother had no intention of stopping her errands, so there could be no enforcement of the limit. Second, the limit—"Behave"—was so general that it gave Alex no room to be himself. What does it mean to *behave?* Children need specific information: "Alex, I am expecting you to *not* run through the stores at the mall when we get there. I know you understand." Third, the earlier threat Alex received ("Alex, I'm warning you") served as a message that in fact his mother expected him to misbehave. Unfortunately, this type of communication creates a challenge and ultimately a powerful struggle. Some parents have difficulty in setting and maintaining any limits on their child's behavior, except in the face of dangerous situations, for fear of being rejected. Their own need to be loved may make it too painful to risk having their child say hurtful things to them. When four-year-old Melanie won't leave the playground after four or five requests, the strongest response her mother can muster is "Please, Melanie, please; you're not being fair." This type of communication is ineffective because it sets no real limits or consequences for the child and won't provide the results the parent is seeking.

At the other extreme are those parents who put too heavy a restriction or too many limits on their child's behavior both at home and outside. The danger in setting too many limits is that such limits will ultimately invite the child to fight and rebel against them, ignore them, or find ways to cheat to get around them. The consequences for a transgression must always be balanced with the transgression's severity. For example, toddlers' obnoxious behaviors such as whining ("Pick me up, pick me up!" or "More, more, more!") are really more annoying than deserving of punishment, so parents need to calmly allow this process to play out. Essentially ignoring the behavior will reinforce the message "I am not going to change my mind, so you need to change your behavior." You may say, for example, "Lucy, I see you want more. I wish you could have more, but the limit is one. You can play here and have fun or you can play in your room. The choice is yours. I see you're angry. You don't like it when I don't give you what you want. I wish you could have more. You make the choice. Play here or in your room."

How you talk to your child during one stage of development will be remembered in the next. The principles, as well as the philosophy that supports these behavioral strides, are based on repetition and patience. These methods of communicating with your child are not intended to work immediately. What will work immediately is starting the child's process of focusing on his own behavior and need for self-control, rather than focusing on the conflict between his parent and himself. That is why a toddler should be given so many chances to make the right decision on his own. Over time, the focus remains on his behavior, not the parent's control. For older children five and up, swift consequences, *not* chances or words, should be given. Consistency is everything.

THE TIME-BREAK METHOD

A key element in setting and maintaining limits is to *not* set a time limit on how long you allow your toddler to complain. "Bobby, quit crying already! Act like a big boy! I'm going to ignore you if you keep complaining! If you keep it up we're not going!" Naturally, it's exhausting and irritating for a parent to listen to such carrying-on. Just as each child has a different tolerance level for frustration, so does each parent. However, allowing toddlers or children to cry, whine, or complain without criticizing or demeaning them will diminish the length of their tantrums or outbursts in the long run.

One way to shorten these spells when a child breaks a limit, assuming you've set a clear rule to begin with, is a swift consequence followed by positive feedback for completing the consequence. Most parents do the opposite: they remind the child again how bad he was and how the punishment will be worse if he does it again. Mistakenly, they believe that more punishment makes the child behave better. Especially for defiant children, you know this is not true. A more effective approach would be: "Cathy, you broke the rule, it's a *time break!*" I suggest these words because the word *timeout* is overused and carries with it baby-behavior feelings, especially for older kids, and unfortunately, timeout has come to mean different things to different children. It's not important how long she stays in her room or is made to stand still for thirty seconds right where she is standing. What is important is that she completes the *time break* successfully. When your child does emerge from her room or the part of the room she was sent to, even if it was for ten or twenty seconds, let her know how well she controlled herself during that time. "Ellen, you could have kicked and screamed more, but you didn't. Thank you for the way you conducted yourself." Look at your child's face when you've finished saying those few words, and you will begin to see a different person emerge. Above all, when you impose a time break, remain calm without any sign of anger. If you do put her in her room, do not shut the door. Simply say, "Danielle, when you calm down, I will be in the living room waiting. I know you can do this."

> When you impose a time break, remain calm without any sign of anger. If you do put her in her room, do not shut the door. Simply say, "Danielle, when you calm down, I will be in the living room waiting. I know you can do this."

Not feeding into your child's disruptive energy pattern should be your predictable response for many long years to come. Having a child take a *break* for a broken limit can happen as frequently as needed. The important part to remember is to be consistent: when a rule is broken, immediately enforce the *time break* consequence. The length of time is not nearly as important as completing the *time break*. Reinforce how successful the child was in completing the *time break*—even if she screamed and kicked, reinforce the positive: "Emily, you really handled that *time break* well! You could have kicked and screamed more, but you controlled yourself. You did it, thank you!" Do not use the one-minute-for-each-year-of-age rule.

Ten seconds, thirty seconds, or one minute will serve the purpose. You may think that such a short break is no consequence
at all, but you will see that the reinforcement of your child's effort and your refusal to feed into his disruptive energy is what
will effect change. I highly recommend Howard Glasser's book,
Transforming the Difficult Child, for practical solutions for those
children who have set a pattern of being defiant and difficult.

KEEP REFLECTING

One way to help prevent a child's meltdown is to quickly reflect, or mirror, the child's feelings, disappointment, and fan-
tasies. If parents reflect their child's state of mind in somewhat
natural and sincere soliloquy, then his bad mood or temper
will likely diminish significantly. For example, you might say,
"Michael, I know you're mad that we have to go now; I know
you're angry at me for taking you away from your toys. It's
time to go but we will be back." Then, after a pause, continue:
"Everything will be here waiting for you when we come back.
I know you want to stay. I see you're angry. We will come
back and visit." In the beginning, this may go on for two, five,
or ten minutes. Michael (although he can't express it yet) will
remember the way you understood his frustration and anger
rather than the enforcement of the consequence. If you do not
empathize with his feelings, he will internalize a repressed inner anger that may erupt at a later time, at which point the parent would say, "I don't understand, it came from nowhere!"
Without authentic empathy from a parent, a child will detach.

Without authentic empathy from a parent, a child will detach.

Ironically, the child's repressed anger would not have been over the disappointment of having been told no, but rather from his feelings of being dismissed and ignored. When you narrate or mirror a child's feelings, the intensity of his outburst is diminished. This is because he feels satisfied in knowing he is at the center of your attention and is understood. Your attitude when reflecting a child's feelings must be sincere and authentic. Children know when something is said gratuitously or falsely, and such insincerity will enrage them more.

It's really no different for adults. You have probably witnessed a bank closing its doors just as a customer arrives. When the security guard says, "I'm sorry, no, I can't let you in," the customer does a little speech dance to persuade the guard to open the door. When this doesn't work, the customer goes further, concocting some story about an emergency or saying that he will be real quick. After these exchanges, you can see the customer becoming more frustrated and angry and unable to accept the guard's answer. This may lead to ranting and raving about how the customer will never use this bank again and will tell his friends not to either. Had the guard simply acknowledged the customer's frustration and anger at the outset, the customer would have in all likelihood accepted the bank staying closed: "I'm sorry. I'm sure you rushed in getting here, but bank policy is all doors must close at four P.M. I understand how disappointed you are." This kind of respect and honest talk is what prevents people from becoming undone. Why is it any different for a child? Early pioneer in social work Leontine Young recognized a child's need to feel respected. "The smaller the person, the less we worry about his dignity. Sometimes we even find the idea a little ludicrous, as if smallness and inexperience were incompatible with anything so majestic as human dignity. . . . Yet children have a great sense of their own dignity. They couldn't define what it is, but they know when it has been violated."

In addition, it is important that when a child transgresses an established limit, the parent's attitude also reflects an unstated *"I know you know better."* Convey confidence in your child. The emphasis should be on both the attitude of the correction and a confidence that you know next time he will do better, even though he probably will transgress. Sometimes just a look or a word can say volumes more than little speeches and can help the child focus on his own behavior. Parents should understand that not all misbehaviors need to be commented on. However, when you do comment, be sure to reject the behavior and *not* the child. Trusting a child to know when he has transgressed aids him in developing his sense of right and wrong and is at the core of what we want him to learn. Of course, consequences must be consistent with what a parent says they will be. Therefore, when a child tries to push through his limits, a parent must still hold to his own.

Parents should understand that not all misbehaviors need to be commented on. However, when you do comment, be sure to reject the behavior and *not* the child.

DON'T THREATEN FIRST!

The importance of *not* talking about punishment before a transgression occurs should be noted here. Talking about consequences beforehand undermines a child's confidence that he'll do the right thing in the first place. A threat of consequences serves as a challenge to a child's autonomy. A parent may say, "Linda, we have to go in five minutes. If you are not ready to leave in five minutes, I'm not taking you to the movies." This type of threat and communication creates a challenge. "Linda, I know you know the rule; we leave in five minutes." Then, if the rule is broken, the challenge, in all likelihood, will become a fight. In contrast, state the rule upfront and not the punishment. A punishment or consequence will not be perceived as heavy-handed. Since the parent gave the child an advanced warning not to do something, and enough time to self-correct, the child understands more clearly that the consequence is a result of her own misbehavior and not a random act of control by the parent.

The confidence in each child to fully comply is steeped in the parent's own belief in him. While there are exceptions, "I can do it" is an attitude that comes not only from the child himself but from the influence of at least one other person. That is why I believe the goal is not to see how *fast* you can get a toddler to stop a misbehavior, but how *long* you give him a chance to *do right*. Toddlers need endless chances, information, and explanations to develop. This is not the same rule for children who are four, five, or six. At those ages, a swift consequence must always follow a transgression. Remember, it is not the punishment that counts but the success the child must feel from completing the consequence. That is why you want the consequence as a rule not to be too punitive.

Again, this might sound like a license for permissiveness, but when consistently communicated, these principles will win over even the most ornery child.

Children Know When They Misbehave

When Sammy, a three-year-old, is throwing his wooden puzzle pieces across the room, his father says, "No, Sammy, don't throw them on the floor." The question is, do you think the toddler didn't know that? Outside of a few misbehaviors, most toddlers and children know when they misbehave. Telling them *no* repeatedly sends the message that they are not smart, and will likely continue, five minutes later, knowing you will be there again with your favorite word, *no,* to stop them. Describing behavior works better: "Looks like you're finished playing with your Legos" or "You must be finished with your sandwich, because you're dropping the bread on the floor." You can also tell the child, "I know you know better."

Observations, statements, or descriptions such as these send the message that you have confidence in the child to stop doing what he's doing. Relentless reprimands reinforce infantile behavior and build no self-confidence or trust between the parent and child. The need for repeated reprimands also means that the parent probably did not enforce the earlier limit that was set. The trick is in allowing your child to expend his own energy while you remain firm but calm, all the while reflecting his mood. This only takes thirty seconds or less, and sooner rather than later, your child will begin to say to himself, "I will find another way."

A constant stream of threats is one of the patterns that contributes to a child's misbehavior. To children, threats are invitations to repeat a prohibited act.

A constant stream of threats is one of the patterns that contributes to a child's misbehavior. To children, threats show a lack of confidence and are invitations to repeat a prohibited act. When a child is told, "If you do it once more . . . ," he does not hear the words "if you." He hears only "a challenge." Most times he interprets it as "My father expects me to do it once more." Such warnings are worse than useless. They ensure that an obnoxious act will be repeated. A warning serves as a challenge to the child's autonomy. If he has any self-respect he must show himself and others he is not afraid by repeating the behavior.

FIVE

Pacifiers

Bitter are the tears of a child: Sweeten them.
Deep are the thoughts of a child: Quiet them.
Sharp is the grief of a child: Take it from him.
Soft is the heart of a child: Do not harden it.

—PAMELA GLENCONNER

Choosing and Starting the Pacifier

Most parents would agree there is a difference between a newborn's involuntary sucking reflex as she searches for food and comfort and a three-year-old's need to suck on a pacifier to reduce anxiety and stave off a tantrum. One is a natural reflexive behavior, the other a learned habit. Parents learn very quickly that giving in to the pacifier habit means more quiet time in the house or car. If I were to ever market my own brand of pacifier, I would package it with this expression: "Plug it in and enjoy the silence!"

Some infants do not have as strong a need to suck as others. They may never take a pacifier. They simply do not use sucking as a means of comforting themselves. But when it is called for, no transitional object is more ubiquitous in our culture than those plastic soothers called pacifiers. In some parts of the English-speaking world, pacifiers are sometimes called dummies; they stand in for the mother's breast, like a dummy stands in for a human being in a department store window. They're available in countless shapes, sizes, colors, and assorted licensed cartoon characters; most toddlers have between three and six, like a Swatch watch collection. Parents know them by different names: pacie, binky, plug, pancake, thing, little friend, wah wah, and more.

Although there is certainly no reason not to introduce your child to a pacifier during early infancy, it is wise *not* to use any cute names when referring to it. Calling it by its real name won't make your child stop in and of itself when the time comes, but it is one more piece to the larger puzzle. Friendly and fun-sounding names reinforce greater infantile behavior and personal attachment.

STARTING

The best time to offer a pacifier is when the infant is searching around with his mouth and trying to suck on anything that is handy. If you notice your infant beginning to suck his fingers or thumbs during the first three months of life, that would be the ideal time to introduce him to a pacifier. As a rule, pacifiers are very helpful for babies who seem to enjoy bottle after bottle of formula, sometimes drinking down more than forty ounces a day. In some studies, premature babies showed increased weight gain when they sucked a pacifier or finger. This extended use seems to indicate that these babies really do need more time sucking. For older infants, who are not really hungry, a pacifier can satisfy this urge without the unnecessary yeast and calories of formula.

Parents should be aware of two problems that can interfere with the healthy use of the pacifier. First, in some cases, parents are reluctant to use it and wait too long, leaving some babies to reject it. The second problem is that when parents continually rely on the pacifier for comforting their child anytime he so much as whimpers, it will eventually become self-defeating for the child. Popping the pacifier into the child's mouth routinely prevents the parent from noticing the subtle signs their child may show signaling he is ready to give it up.

No parent would think twice about a fourteen-month-old using a pacifier. The question of age appropriateness is really the central issue with pacifiers. How old is *too* old? And how long is *too* long for such behavior? Every experienced parent would agree that a baby who has routine periods of crankiness can be completely quieted with a pacifier to suck. With regard to age appropriateness, a three- or four-year-old should *not* be sporting a pacifier or bottle in his mouth. More to the point, pacifier, bottle, and thumb use should not extend beyond the first twenty months or so. That's not to say that those children who continue this habit beyond that time are at any real developmental risk—they're not; however, prolonging this habit will certainly contribute to a delay in behavioral maturity. Even a three-year-old can doubt she's getting "bigger" when feeling the need to suck on a plastic pacifier or her thumb each time she is confronted by a frustrating moment or an oncoming tantrum.

Even a three-year-old can doubt she's getting "bigger" when feeling the need to suck on a plastic pacifier or her thumb each time she is confronted by a frustrating moment or an oncoming tantrum.

Experienced parents know firsthand how the relentless screaming and whining for a pacifier in the middle of the night can make any sleep-deprived adult a little cranky. Add to that bumping your face into a wall or stubbing your toe on the nightstand as you search in the darkness for that *thing* is enough to, well . . . undo anyone. However, the ability to help your child through those moments (with more than just throwing the object across the room) can help him stop that habit more easily when the proper time comes. In the meantime, as you hand your screaming child his favorite object and say with a reassuring voice, "You were looking for your pacifier, Andy. There . . . that feels better," it allows your child to include *you* and not just the object in his comforting. That might not sound like much, but to your child, it is proof that you are in tune with his anxious feelings. It is all those anxious moments repeated over and over again during those first twenty months that build an impenetrable trust between you and your child when the times comes to stop a habit. If reflecting back your two- or three-year-old's feelings sounds overly simplistic in getting your child to *listen and abide,* it is not. Trust and empathy, the essential cornerstones in building up the parent-child relationship, must come before change. Earnestly reflect back your child's discontent by saying, "You don't like it that you don't have your pacifier. You're angry at me for not finding you another one. Sometimes it's hard to stop crying," helps reduce his anxiety. This honest and respectful run-on soliloquy (you can add more!) allows your child to sense a degree of attunement. It is not meant to stop the habit instantly. It is meant to build dialogue and trust that over time will be the basis for a new kind of shorthand. This style of communication is *not* a one-time way of talking! It must be part of your permanent repertoire. These two building blocks (trust and empathy) will relax a child, so he can hear what you have to say even though he might resist. With consistency, this kind of dialogue will lead to a new behavior and a new kind of *self-control* for your child. Parents must be diligent in understanding the difference between accepting a child's feelings and accepting his behavior. Bad feelings are always tolerated, bad behavior is not!

CHOOSING A PACIFIER

If your baby uses pacifiers, she will invariably have a collection of them, perhaps as many as six or more. I highly recommend not choosing one with a licensed cartoon character that your child sees on television each day. Six months or a year from now, when you will want your child to quit, that licensed character (especially if it's the same one he is watching on television) has a way of extending dependency. Each character has its own reinforcing personality, which may contribute to the behavior you are trying to stop. (Additional pitfalls associated with licensed cartoon characters are discussed in chapter ten.) Putting aside pacifier fashion for the moment, the following are some considerations to keep in mind when choosing a pacifier:

- To avoid improper breathing, choose a pacifier that does not extend over the nostril.

- Choose a nipple shape that resembles the mother's natural nipple and breast. This is especially important if the child started out being breast-fed.
- Your infant grows quickly, so check the guard shield every few months to make sure that it is large enough not to fit in his mouth.
- Make sure that the guard shield is ventilated with holes.
- Never make a do-it-yourself pacifier using a bottle nipple.

Pacifier Safety

When it comes to pacifiers, moderation is key. Do your best to avoid having a child walk around with one in his mouth for hours on end each day, and by all means do not let him use the pacifier around the clock. A pacifier constantly in the mouth can be hazardous once your child becomes active and is more apt to fall. Moreover, pacifiers can cause abnormal development of the jaws and teeth, depending on the age of the child. Reasons for this could be improper size and shape of the pacifier, strength of sucking action, and length of time the pacifier is in the mouth. Also, replace the pacifier every two or three months, due to possible wear and tear (holes in nipples, sticky latex, nipple deteriorated from saliva, heat damage, sunlight discoloration, and bacterial buildup). As a rule, the clear rubber nipple is better than the yellow: it lasts longer.

PACIFIERS IN THE BED

If your baby is still on the pacifier after five or six months and awakes several times a night because he loses it in the crib, put several in his bed at bedtime so that there's a better chance of his finding one by himself. The other alternative is a glow-in-the-dark pacifier. In any case, never put a long cord on a pacifier to hang it around the baby's neck or tie it to the crib bar. This can be extremely dangerous, as the cord can become wrapped around the baby's finger, wrist, or neck.

REPLACE OLD PACIFIERS

When a baby has a few teeth, he can pull the nipple of an old, tired pacifier off the disk or chew pieces out of the nipple. These pieces may cause choking, especially if swallowed the wrong way. So, buy new pacifiers when the old ones become too pasty. Pacifiers can become contaminated with candida, a species of yeastlike fungi. If your baby develops thrush—a yeast infection in the mouth—you'll want to sterilize the pacifier by placing it in boiling water for ten minutes—or better yet, throw it away.

Physical Effects of Pacifier Use

A brochure recently published by the American Academy of Pediatric Dentistry (AAPD) cautions that extended pacifier usage can cause the upper front teeth to tip toward the lip. Pacifiers, however, are less likely to cause such a malocclusion and are usually discontinued at an earlier age than thumb suck-ing—it is easier to take away a pacifier than a finger or thumb. But as with any product a child ingests or places in his or her mouth, it is better to understand the patterns of behavior that can develop from both short- or long-term use. Here are some general guidelines:

- Buy a pacifier with a nipple made of rubber to avoid any trauma or infection to the gums. (I have seen parents give their young infants a piece of thick plastic to suck on!)
- In rare instances, pacifiers may cause complications such as abnormal swallowing patterns.
- Check the pacifier daily for breakage. They do not last for-ever. The child could suck a damaged pacifier and choke on a portion of it.
- Some articles have suggested that *overuse* of the pacifier con-tributed to more frequent ear infections. It is the *overuse* that is the danger, far more than the pacifier itself. Parents should do their best to restrict anytime use of pacifiers to effectively reduce the chances of acute ear inflammation.

THRUSH

Thrush is a yeast infection of the lining of the mouth. White patches in and around the mouth are the main symptoms. Thrush always involves the sides of the mouth and the tongue, and sometimes the lips. Unlike milk, these white patches can-not be wiped away. Thrush is caused by a yeast called *Candida albicans.* Yeast is found in just about everyone's mouth and intestinal tract, and it normally doesn't invade tissue unless the tissue has been damaged, as can occur from prolonged sucking on a bottle or pacifier. Also, the recent use of antibiotics can decrease the mouth's natural resistance to yeast infections by killing off the good bacteria. If your baby has a diaper rash at the same time as thrush, it may well be caused by the same yeast and require Lotrimin, Nystatin, or other yeast cream. Similarly, if you are breast-feeding and are experiencing pain or redness around your nipples, the culprit may be yeast.

Decrease Friction

The key to preventing recurrences of thrush is cutting back on friction to the lining of the mouth. Keep bottle-sucking time to no more than twenty minutes per feeding and eliminate the pacifier temporarily until the thrust is cured. If your infant is using an orthodontic pacifier, switch to a smaller, regular one. Bigger ones can irritate the mouth more. Once the thrush is cured, your baby can return to her pacifier, but try not to let her use it more than an hour per day.

Sterilize Bottle Nipples and Pacifiers

Sterilize or replace any bottle nipples or pacifiers, since they are likely to be contaminated with yeast. Once thrush has cleared, the pacifiers and nipples don't need to be boiled, as yeast can't cause any trouble in a normal mouth.

Take Medication

To eradicate thrush, your baby may need a prescription medicine called Mycostatin or Nystatin Suspension. Call your pediatrician. These liquid medicines can be applied directly on the areas of thrush with a cotton swab. They can also be placed in the mouth with a dropper, but one must be careful to keep the drops in the front of the mouth—if it's placed in the back of the mouth and swallowed, it doesn't do any good. Also, don't feed your baby anything for thirty minutes or more after application of the Nystatin.

Watch Eating Patterns

Though pacifiers are widely used to calm fussy babies and weary parents, mothers should be aware that pacifier use can affect both the initiation and duration of the breast-feeding relationship.

> **Though pacifiers are widely used to calm fussy babies and weary parents, mothers should be aware that pacifier use can affect both the initiation and duration of the breast-feeding relationship.**

In a serious 1992 study, pacifier use before two weeks of age resulted in babies sucking incorrectly at the breast. This in turn caused a shorter duration of breast-feeding. It was further determined that there was a threefold risk of early weaning from the breast in babies who used a pacifier. Sucking is very important for babies, and pacifier use takes away from the time the infant spends at the breast. With the baby spending less time at the breast, the mother's prolactin production then decreases, which compromises her milk supply. Insufficient milk supply can interfere with the proper nutrition and growth of the baby. Parents should try to avoid the introduction of pacifiers in the first four to six weeks of breast-feeding. Pacifiers are sometimes used indiscriminately—popped into the baby's mouth regardless of not only his feeding cues but also his other needs. Instead, he may need to be fed, held, rocked, or changed. Using a pacifier to take care of every difficulty, a parent may begin to lose touch with the baby's real needs. We need to look at each individual baby and determine his particular needs.

There are times when pacifier use can be helpful to the baby, such as when mother and baby are separated: while a mother is at work, the baby is unable to meet his sucking needs at the breast. At such times, the pacifier can be very calming to him. Because each baby's needs should be evaluated on an individual basis, it is impossible to recommend a particular time when it is "safe" to begin use of a pacifier. If you decide that a pacifier is appropriate for your baby, it is important to watch him for any changes. If the use of a pacifier reduces your baby's frequency or duration of feeds (newborns should be nursing at least eight to twelve times a day) or makes it difficult for him to feed at the breast, discontinue its use. During your baby's first two months, you should allow the baby to nurse as much as she needs. Your milk supply by that time is probably finely tuned to her needs, and she may be taking longer at each feed to get the amount of milk she needs. Keep an eye on her output. She should be wetting five to six diapers each day and having regular, substantial bowel movements. Regular weight checks will also help you to be sure she is getting all the milk she needs. Normal weight gain for babies under four months of age is four to eight ounces per week. If she falls short in either of these areas, I would recommend saving pacifier use for times of real necessity, such as during her moody times in the car or when putting her down before a nap or for bedtime.

How to Stop the Pacifier Habit

It is important to keep in mind that removing the pacifier *too* early may affect your child's ability to satisfy his sucking needs, which later may prevent him from developing the capacity to soothe himself. Certainly, you do not want to stop his use of a pacifier before thirteen months just because you know it can become an obnoxious habit later on. I suggest stopping the habit at eighteen months; do not let it go beyond your child's second birthday. When you're ready to begin this process, it is wise to have his favorite soft toy waiting in the wings. Effecting change, like all behavior, is dynamic. While some behaviors are predictable, others are not. What may work well with one child may have to be slightly modified to work with another.

Just the thought of taking away your child's pacifier can make you want to delay the inevitable. As you prepare yourself for this new mission, remember to set and manage your expectations first. This is the secret, as it is with all behaviors you are working on to change. Prepare yourself for the range of emotions and reactions your child will show. This alone will decrease your stress level and your child's. And finally, repeat to yourself, "I can do this"—and you know what . . . you can!

GETTING READY FOR THE BIG CHANGE

By the time your toddler is about eighteen to twenty months, he is likely to be ready to make the transition to stop the pacifier habit. As with all developmental behavior, there will be conflicting urges. A part of your child wants to remain infantile while another and stronger part wants to strive for independence and autonomy.

Before beginning this process, I highly recommend reading my children's storybook *Binky Blastoff! The Final Countdown*. It prepares your child in an honest and active way to stop the pacifier habit. The story is packed with visual images and physical activity to help your child prepare for what he is about to do. It provides the child with a real sense of control. Read it once each day for five consecutive days before removing all the pacifiers from the house and from under the seats of your car. Reading *Binky Blastoff! will* accelerate your child's success. You can find it at www.parentfitness.com.

There is much we can do and say as parents to teach a child self-regulation without reaching for a pacifier. As tempting as it may be to put a pacifier in the mouth to quiet a screaming two-year-old, the message this action sends is confusing at best: "Quiet yourself down and suck on a pacifier like a baby!" At the same time, this is also the stage when your child may be engaged in the daily practice of potty training, which is a declaration of getting older. Reinforcing expressions to encourage

big boy or big girl behavior is in direct contradiction to pacifier use. Your child is likely to find herself caught between two
competing worlds. If we are to help a child *act* bigger, we must
first start with helping a child *feel* bigger. Remember, children
still derive a significant part of their self-image from interact-
ing with their parents. The reactions and influence of a par-
ent(s) remain dominant in their psyches. Children will live up
to your image of them, so you must think twice before sticking
a pacifier in a child's mouth or belittling his behavior with expressions like "Okay already, here's your baby pacie."

One of the more effective ways to communicate with your
child is to be direct. Many parents feel they are, but unfortunately, part of that "directness" includes name calling, comparisons, and promoting a general feeling about the child's bad
habit that makes him feel "bad" about himself. The direct approach is *not* a license to bark out orders and instructions. You
want to be sure that you are not yelling and bullying when you
are helping change a child's behavior. Parents need to express
authentic empathy with expressions such as "I know you miss
your pacifier, you wish it was back." This will help build trust
between you and your child. This approach should not be confused with maintaining your strict limit. Physically taking the
pacifier is the easy part. Your words must be free of humiliation. One of my favorite Wordwear T-shirts says it best: "Caution: Some Words May Cause Side Effects."

Just like an adult, a small child needs time to prepare for
change. I recommend giving a kind of heads-up casual news
flash with the information you want her to have. "Samantha, in
three minutes we are leaving the house to go to the store. You

can use your pacifier until then, but then it must remain in the house. When we return, it will be here for you. Let me know you understand?" Asking that question at the end serves to bring the child into the moment. Children will adjust easier to new changes if you tell them in advance. This applies to most situations that include a nagging anxiety about some future event. For bigger issues, like stopping a pacifier habit, you should announce these changes to your child at least three to five days in advance. For some reason, parents feel that talking about a future change of plans, such as going away on a trip, canceling a planned outing, going to the doctor, or being dropped off with friends or relatives should be brought up at the last minute to minimize a child's anxiety. Not so. Telling a child in advance of something important also tells him that you believe in him to make the adjustment. It is a long-term parenting philosophy.

> **Children will adjust easier to new changes if you tell them in advance. For bigger issues, like stopping a pacifier habit, you should announce these changes to your child at least three to five days in advance.**

THE THREE-DAY METHOD

When considering the pacifier habit, think of it in terms of a countdown. I suggest that you give your child three days' advance notice about no longer being able to use his pacifier. If all goes according to plan, soon your child will be pacifier free! As you prepare yourself for this seemingly daunting task, your attitude must be one of calm and casualness. You want to instill in your child the confidence that you have that he will be okay without his pacifier. Just as important, you want to continue to remind yourself about the likely tirade to follow. Be unrelenting. You will get through it. When you first tell your child the news that his pacifier days are coming to an end, in all likelihood he will not react with the ferocious resistance you might expect. The reason is quite simple: in your child's mind, this plan is a long way off!

Finally, choose a time to talk with your child when he is feeling relaxed and pleased with himself. Be sure you do not pick a time when he is tired or going to bed, or when he is parked in front of the television with the pacifier in his mouth. The pacifier-sucking habit is not such a painful habit to break; more painful is the parent having to endure her child's crying and whining. Although it can appear that taking the pacifier away will be traumatic for your child, I can assure you it is not. The entire process is totally dependent on your leadership. You must be sure you build his confidence that he can do without it. Never let him feel with your soothing tone that he is falling apart and can't handle being without his pacifier. Never say, "Poor little boy," or use platitudes like, "There, there, Michael, it will be better," or belittling expressions such as "Cut it out, you're acting like a baby." Give him confidence and encouragement through your facial expressions and words. Use expressions like "I know this is hard. I know you can do this."

These are not magic words that will make all the whining go away; they are words to make the helpless feelings go away. You must repeat and repeat and repeat, but it will work!

Remember, the talk you have with your toddler is not a lecture. Lectures raise anxiety levels and produce glazed-over eyes. Your talk should not be more than thirty seconds. If you can't say it clearly in thirty seconds, don't! Collect your thoughts and rehearse until you can say it in thirty seconds or less.

> **Lectures raise anxiety levels and produce glazed-over eyes. Your talk should not be more than thirty seconds. If you can't say it clearly in thirty seconds, don't! Collect your thoughts and rehearse until you can say it in thirty seconds or less.**

Parents generally go into far too much detail with lessons, lectures, and over-the-top stories with their children when they want them to stop certain behaviors. Be succinct. Your thirty-second description of the plan should sound like casual information about what's to come. In fact, the thirty-second rule applies to most communication involving negative news or a new limit or rule. "Daniel, next week I have to go out of town on a business meeting. I will be in San Diego. I'll be back in two days." Your tone and facial expression are calm and informal. The key is not to make a moment into an event! Whatever follow-up questions your child asks, remain calm and answer the questions with a reassuring smile. The underlying principle of calm directness is something you will want to use throughout these parent-guidance years. Talking in a direct way shows respect—no tricking, no distractions, no elaborate, apologetic made-up stories. This should not mean your emotions are flat. A caring tone is *always* front and center.

> **The length of time it takes for your child to accept what you say is largely dependent on your style of communicating. "Talking up" to a child really means talking *with* him. It means not talking down to him, not talking at him, and not ignoring what he is saying.**

The length of time it takes for your child to accept what you say is largely dependent on your style of communicating. "Talking up" to a child really means talking *with* him. It means not talking down to him, not talking at him, and not ignoring what he is saying. It is talking with a genuine faith that your child knows you believe in him and that he can do it! Talking up to a child will feel more relaxed and natural for you as well, and is *less* taxing. It takes more energy to talk down to your child than it does to talk *with* him.

The next step is to stop any baby talk or using pet names. "Lilly, where's your pacie?" "Does Bobby Boo want more baba?" Some parents add the suffix *y* to their child's first name: "Good boy, Mikey"; "Put it here, Greggy." Many parents actually call their toddlers by the name Baby instead of their real name: "Baby, do you want something to eat?" Although this may sound cute and loving to the parent, the toddler hears this differently. For a toddler, baby talk reinforces the feeling that she is still a infant. The toddler will mimic the baby talk instead of learning real words, which conflicts with her own nat-

ural maturity and autonomy. This is a time for rapid vocabulary expansion: although the toddler's speaking vocabulary
may be limited, her listening vocabulary is extensive! If baby
talk continues into the toddler years, behavioral maturity will
almost always be delayed.

Day One

Prescription:

Twice a day/30 seconds each morning and bedtime

When you find the right moment, in a *slow* manner say,
"Michael, I would like to tell you something. I can see how
you want to do a lot of things that make you older. That's a
good idea. I can see you're ready to start. In three days it will
be time to say good-bye to *all* your pacifiers. In three days it
will be time to stop using all of them. I know you understand.
We will do this together." Wait for his reaction, and *if* there is
one, whatever he says, reflect it back. That's it. The whole talk
should take thirty seconds. Do not give any impression that
you are seeking his approval or permission. Use the same delivery as you would if you were telling him of an upcoming
trip to the park. Typically, you will get back just a nod or a
certain look that lets you know he got the message. You should
talk in a way that shows you have confidence in him to make
this work. Do not make the moment into an event! Later that
night when he asks for his pacifier, remind him again about
your earlier talk: "Michael, remember our talk this morning
about giving up the pacifier? I can see how you want to do a
lot of things that make you older. That's a good idea. In three
days it will be time to say good-bye to *all* your pacifiers. In

three days it will be time to stop using all of them. I know you understand. We will do this together." Wait for his reaction, and *if* there is one, whatever he says, reflect it back. That's it. Then along with your normal routine, if he asks for his pacifier, give it to him.

That was day one. So far, so good!

Day Two

Prescription:
Twice a day/30 seconds each morning and bedtime

Day two should be essentially a repeat of day one. Whatever fuss he may make, stay with your message and just reflect his feelings as you continue with your plan. Do not sell him on the idea; it will only challenge and anger him more. Do not engage or be drawn into any long conversations. The key is few words and more reflection.

That was day two.

Day Three

As this is the day you are physically going to gather up all his pacifiers, you will want to make sure you have put aside about twenty to thirty minutes. You can do this either in the morning or afternoon. Begin by telling him directly and calmly, "Michael, today is the third day. It is time to gather up all your pacifiers." If you have read *Binky Blastoff!* remind him of the story. Use the concept of self-talk (a kind of thinking out loud): "Mmmmm, I wonder how many rooms they are in?" To be fair, he really won't be able to supply the answer, but you can be sure he understands the question and what will happen. It will be another reminder about the talk you had a few days ago, and it will help make him an active partner. If he does complain, which in all likelihood he will, continue to reflect back with a strong sense of empathy, your understanding that he does not want to do this: "Michael, you don't feel like stopping the pacifier now." Do not engage in any selling of the idea or talking about how much older he will feel without it. You must maintain a quiet and relaxed confidence both in yourself and him, that he can go through this. "Michael, you can do this. I know you understand"; "You're ready now." Talk in fifteen-second sound bites—that's it. Let him watch you go from room to room finding his pacifiers. It should be done in a relaxed way, *not* punitively. Think of it in terms of casually going into his room and picking up his clothes and toys, which you probably do anyway. Be sure to reflect whatever feelings he is expressing, but *be unwavering about sticking to the plan.*

As you walk around finding each pacifier, place them one by one into a small plastic bag. Try to enlist your child's help, but if he does not want to help, that's okay too. Keep going. Don't forget to also look in the backseat of your car or SUV. As you do this, keep the energy high, with the fun feeling that you are on a scavenger hunt. Keep the momentum going with commentary like "Mmmm, I wonder how many we'll find in our car?" Do not do a lot of talking. Assuming your child has been watching you do this, let him see you place the pacifiers one at a time into the plastic bag. It would be even more effective if your child actually places some of them in the bag with you. This will mark a turning point, as he sees this is for real. Remind him: "Remember our talk about the three days." During this exchange, be sure *not* to sound like you're asking for permission to do this. If your child is having a crying tantrum, say: "You don't like that I remembered the three days. You wish I had forgotten. You wish there was more time left."

As you finish placing the last pacifier into the bag, tell him that you will be sending them to a special place called a recycling center. That is where plastics and rubber are kept to make other things, like toys, plastic plates, and even parts for cars. Then walk to the front door of your house or apartment and leave the bag outside. Tell him you are leaving them by the door because someone will pick them up. (Obviously, that someone is you.) Use the next minute or so to explain about the recycling process and the special machinery involved in pounding and pulverizing. Also let your child know that when you pass a recycling drop-off center on the road (at supermarkets, etc.), you will be sure to point one out for him to see. This conversation, while upsetting to him, is also calming because of the interesting new information and details he is acquiring. He may look or act like he is tuning out, but he is tuning in. Remember, your child's listening vocabulary is at least fifty times greater than his speaking vocabulary. Many parents in the middle of this plan just dump the pacifiers in the garbage. I do not recommend that. You will get much more mileage out of the recycling story for days and weeks ahead than letting your child see them dumped into the garbage can.

Within a few minutes, when your child is out of sight, you should retrieve the bag of pacifiers and really put them in the recycling bin at your house or apartment. If you do have the time and patience, and really want to complete the process impeccably, put your child in the car and drive together to a recycling drop-off center. At the same time, if it is not possible or practical, just throw them away.

That's it.

I can assure you that within forty-eight hours or *less* your child will be finished with the pacifier habit. Try not to cave in by keeping one pacifier in reserve. This plan will work! As with pulling off a Band-Aid, the slower you pull, the more pain. Don't be surprised if during the next few months, as you pass a recycling drop-off center, he remarks, "Look—my binkies are in there." Acknowledge this, and assure him that you remember. If your child wants his pacifier back, don't be baited into a contest of wills: in a calm and patient way, just repeat the information about what you both knew would happen and did happen. Your child may well appear upset, but he will also feel safe in how you delivered a review of your plan.

Although the direct Three-Day Method is best, here are seven other quick ideas that can work too:

PLAY "PILLOW WISH"

To your child, say, "Do you sometimes wish for things? Me too. Sometimes they come true and sometimes they don't. Sometimes they can happen when we don't expect them. Daniel, you know how sometimes you wish you didn't need your pacifier? Well, tonight we'll play pillow wish." Then have the child place all of his pacifiers under his pillow at night. Be sure he helps somewhat in locating them and placing them there.

When he wakes up, the pacifiers are gone, replaced by a new toy or other plaything he has been wanting. Be sure to tell your child in advance about the wishing game, and be sure the chosen toy is a real surprise. When your child asks for the pacifiers back during moments of frustration, acknowledge his feelings, but remind him of the game: "You're missing your pacifier—even though you are happy with your wish, sometimes that can happen."

SNIPPETY SNIP

Out of sight of your child, snip off the end of the pacifier nipple. Then, before she asks for her pacifier, show her how dangerous the rubber has become: "Look, Rebecca—look at the rubber tip. That's called jagged. Can you say *jagged*? This sure can be dangerous and make the rubber taste funny." Explain that the damaged pacifier is too dangerous to keep and that the other pacifiers are also a danger, even though they have not torn yet. Show genuine concern and surprise. If possible, have the child herself throw the pacifier in the trash can. If the child demands to be bought a new one, in a calm but reassuring tone tell her that it is time to buy a cup and that she can pick it out. If she insists on wanting a pacifier, accept that feeling, but repeat that it's time now for a cup. Don't personalize it by saying that it is time for *her* to grow up and act older. This can sound degrading and sets up a challenge. Be realistic; this will take many rounds. Be firm but understanding.

THE LIMIT RULE

Using limits to modify behavior has many variations. You could limit pacifier use to certain rooms and keep decreasing the number of rooms in which use is allowed until there are none left. Begin by not allowing use anywhere but home. Or try a time limitation—let's say five minutes in certain rooms— or permit usage only at nap time and bedtime, and eventually only bedtime.

THE FULL TUMMY/FULL SCHEDULE

It may seem obvious, but a tired or hungry child is more apt to feel insecure and be less equipped to deal well with stressful situations. Eat frequent, healthy meals, do projects, or engage in any other physical activity that keeps the child's hands busy. The longer he goes, the less dependent he becomes. This is more tiring for the parent but it is effective.

THE CUP PRIZE

Play any simple game at home and let your child know that if she wins, she gets a prize—a new sippy cup! Take her to the store to buy it! Show what it looks like and leave it out each day so she can look at it or play with it. It will become more familiar as well as a motivating target when you talk about stopping with the pacifier.

THE NIGHT PLAN

Explain to her that you expect her to give up the pacifier in three days. Then give her some options: "After you fall asleep, would you like me to come in your room and slip it out of your mouth, or would you like to try one night a week without it?" Your goal is to cultivate your child's interest in giving up her dependable pacifier. If she comes up with a plan, you'll need to assist her in following through with it.

THE "LET IT BE" PLAN

Let him have the pacifier for bedtime. Your bet is that sometime prior to his taking his driver's test, he'll say, "Yeah, I guess I'm done!"

SIX

Bottles

Children equate talking *slowly* and
taking your time with trust.

—MARK BRENNER

Choosing and Starting with the Right Bottle

Once you have made your decision to bottle-feed your baby, do not waste your limited energy feeling guilty. Your child's life, twenty years from today, will not hold more promise if you had breast-fed or bottle-fed longer! If you want to start bottle-feeding after your initial breast-feeding, it's important to remember that your infant is still not old enough to live just on cereal or juice. She needs at least four to six milk feedings a day. So, if you are aiming to wean her from the breast completely, you'll need to get her used to taking a bottle of formula (not juice) before you even begin to cut down her breast-feedings, then gradually replace one with the other. She may take pumped breast milk better than formula, or one formula more readily than another. Trial and error is the only way to really approach this transition. Finally, you should consider allowing someone else to give her the bottle during this transition. She will almost certainly take it better from someone who, unlike you, doesn't smell of breast milk. If she refuses the bottle completely, there's nothing you can do but accept it, breast-feed her, and try again in a couple of days.

One of the least-discussed situations regarding bottle-fed

babies is their need to keep sucking after finishing a bottle. A baby cannot go on sucking on a bottle for comfort after she has finished sucking for food, the way she can at the breast—the lack of air remaining in the bottle won't permit it. There are, however, a couple of options for satisfying the need to suck. First, you could check on how long it is taking your child to drink all the formula she wants. If she is emptying the bottle or getting full in ten minutes or so, check how fast the formula is coming out of the nipple when you turn over the bottle. If it drips out at more than three drops per second, it would be worth trying a nipple with a slightly smaller hole so that she can suck a little longer and harder to get the milk. Don't go crazy, though: milk must drip out of the nipple when the bottle is overturned, and too small a hole in the nipple will frustrate your baby and ultimately lead her to stop feeding before she gets enough to eat. If the baby has had all the sucking she can get from feeding and is still crying, try offering her a finger to suck instead of a pacifier. If she stops crying and sucks on it, that tells you it's more sucking she wants. Your finger is one solution; a pacifier may be another.

CHOOSING THE RIGHT BOTTLE

Babies can be fussy about their personal preferences, so you may need to experiment a bit before settling on one type of bottle. You may also want to take notice of the ergonomics of design. Many manufacturers now offer bottles that are curved in the middle, which makes holding them very comfortable. There are many claims as to which bottle and nipple design will best prevent colic, gas, and other stomach upsets caused by air getting into your baby's tummy during feedings.

Here are a few pointers to keep in mind when choosing a bottle, along with some items and quantity suggestions:

Make sure you purchase enough bottles and related gear.
- four to six four-ounce bottles
- six to eight eight-ounce bottles
- eight to ten nipple-cap-hood sets
- one bottle and nipple brush
- one insulated bag and cold pack
- the appropriate basket for your dishwasher

Avoid glass baby bottles.

Glass bottles are not only breakable, they're not recommended for use with breast milk—the antibodies in breast milk tend to cling to the glass, thereby depriving your baby of one of mother's milk's most vital properties.

Disposable-style bottles are not necessarily better.

Bottles with plastic liners to hold the formula may appear to be more convenient from a cleaning standpoint, but they cost more and require more assembly time. However, if you are nursing and bottle-feeding, the liners are the perfect size for storing expressed breast milk.

Bottle Safety

The American Academy of Pediatric Dentistry has developed the following guidelines for a baby's safe bottle use:

- Never allow a child to fall asleep with a bottle containing milk, formula, fruit juices, or other sweet liquids.
- Never let a child run with a bottle in her mouth.
- Comfort a child who wants a bottle between regular feedings or during naps with a bottle filled with cool water.
- Always make sure a child's bottle is clean, and never dip the nipple in a sweet liquid.
- Introduce children to a cup as they approach one year of age. Children should begin to prepare to stop drinking from a bottle soon after their first birthday.
- Avoid too much milk. Typically infants drink up to thirty-two ounces a day, according to many pediatricians. Toddlers only need two or three servings of dairy a day, equivalent to sixteen to twenty-four ounces of milk. While milk is a healthy food, kids who drink too much of it may not want to eat enough solid food, and they will miss out on important nutrients like iron.

In addition, according to the American Academy of Pediatrics, sterilization of bottles and nipples is no longer necessary as long as you use a municipal water supply (as opposed to using well water) and have a dishwasher. Some formula manufacturers continue to recommend that you boil water for about a minute before mixing it with powder and concentrate, especially for younger babies. Check with your pediatrician to be on the safe side.

USE AND STORAGE

Once you've diluted powder formula with water, you must keep it refrigerated and use it within twenty-four to forty-eight hours. It's best—and economical—to mix only what you need, the guideline being not more than a baby can consume in a day. Cans of ready-to-feed formula must also be refrigerated and covered once opened. Discard whatever isn't eaten within forty-eight hours. If you have to transport opened or mixed formula, always keep it in an insulated bag with a cold pack until you're ready to serve it. Premixed formula that's been left unrefrigerated for more than four hours must be discarded, and experts also recommend that you throw out any formula left in a bottle that your baby hasn't finished within an hour of when he first took the bottle. For this reason, it's better to start out with a less-than-full bottle—you can always add more if your baby still seems hungry, but you can't save what he doesn't finish.

Physical and Emotional Side Effects of Bottle Use

Every parent knows the love affair between baby and bottle and the security it brings. But most pediatricians recommend that parents start weaning their children off the bottle around twelve or fourteen months to avoid a possible bigger problem later called baby-bottle tooth decay.

BABY-BOTTLE TOOTH DECAY

Baby-bottle tooth decay, or nursing-bottle mouth, is a leading dental problem for children under three years of age. Baby-bottle tooth decay occurs when a child's teeth are exposed to sugary liquids, such as formula, fruit juices, and other sweetened liquids, for an extended period of time. If the bottle contains anything other than water, what you have is an acidic solution that is washing over the teeth and decalcifying them, which can lead to cavities. The sugary liquid flows over the baby's upper front teeth and dissolves the enamel, causing decay that can lead to infection. The practice of putting a baby to bed with a bottle, which the baby can suck on for hours, is the major cause of this dental condition. The longer the practice continues, the greater the damage to the baby's teeth and mouth. Treatment can be very expensive.

How to Stop the Bottle Habit

The method for stopping the bottle habit is virtually the same as that for stopping the pacifier habit. Just the thought of taking away your child's bottle can make you want to delay the inevitable. You're probably already visualizing your child and hearing his screaming voice in your head: "I want my baba! Where's baba!" Then . . . a full-blown meltdown. As you prepare yourself for this new mission, remember to set and manage your expectations first. This is the secret, as it is with establishing all new desired behaviors. Prepare yourself for the range of emotions and reactions your child will show. This alone will decrease your stress level as well as your child's. And finally, repeat to yourself, "I can do this"—because you can!

GETTING READY FOR THE BIG CHANGE

By the time babies are between twelve and eighteen months old, they're often ready to make the transition from bottle to cup. At this age, they're becoming more interested in what's going on around them than they are in being confined to sucking on a bottle. However, phasing out the bottle means planning ahead. Here are some tips for early planning:

- Starting at about ten months, let your child occasionally drink from a sippy cup, so when you eventually do get rid of the bottle, he will already be acquainted with the cup.
- Let babies get used to a cup while they're in their crib. They can play with it, fill it with toys, and take the top off.
- Don't always put juice in a cup and milk in a bottle. If you get him used to this association, your child may refuse to drink milk from a cup.

Before beginning this process, I highly recommend reading my children's storybook *Bottle Bowling! A Fun Way to Put the Bottles Away.* It prepares your child in an honest and active way to stop the bottle habit. The story is packed with visual images and physical activity to help him prepare for what he is about to do. It provides the child with a real sense of control. Read it once each day for five consecutive days before you start removing all the bottles from the house and from under the seats of your car. Reading *Bottles Down!* will accelerate your child's success. You can find the book at www.parentfitness.com.

Also, it is important to keep in mind that removing the bottle *too* early may affect your child's ability to satisfy his sucking needs, which later may prevent him from developing the capacity to soothe himself. Certainly, you do not want to stop his use of a bottle before thirteen months just because you know it can become an obnoxious habit later on.

> **It is important to keep in mind that removing the bottle *too* early may affect your child's ability to satisfy his sucking needs, which later may prevent him from developing the capacity to soothe himself.**

When you're ready to begin this process, it is wise to have your child's favorite cuddly or toy standing by. Effecting change, like all behavior, is dynamic. While some behaviors are predictable, others are not. What may work well with one child may have to be slightly modified to work with another. However, the underlying principles of mutual respect and allowing for process go unchanged.

Having said that, one of the best ways to communicate with your child is to be direct. Many parents feel they are, but unfortunately, part of that "directness" includes name calling, comparisons, and a general feeling about the child's habit that makes him feel "bad." The direct approach is *not* a license to bark out orders and instructions. You want to be sure that you are not yelling and bullying your way through when helping your child stop a habit. Parents need to express authentic empathy with expressions like: "I know you miss your bottle, you wish it was back." This will help build trust between you and your child. This approach should not be confused with maintaining your strict limit. Physically taking the bottle is the easy part. Your words must be free of humiliation. One of my favorite Word-wear T-shirts says it best: "Caution: Some Words May Cause Side Effects."

Just like an adult, a small child needs time to prepare for change. For example, this preparation could include not allow-ing a child to take his favorite toy in the car (because there is no time to find it, or it is too big, or any number of other rea-sons). I recommend giving a kind of heads-up news flash be-fore saying no. "Ellen, in three minutes we are leaving the house to go to the store. You can have your bottle until then, but it must remain in the house. When we return, it will be here for you. I know you understand? Let me know you un-derstand." Asking the question at the end serves to bring the child into the moment. Children will adjust easier to new changes if you tell them in advance. This applies to most situ-ations that involve nagging anxiety about some future event. For bigger issues, like stopping a baby-bottle habit, you should announce these changes to your child at least three to five days in advance.

Children will adjust easier to new changes if you tell them in advance. For bigger issues, like stopping a baby-bottle habit, you should announce these changes at least three to five days in advance.

For some reason parents feel that talking about going away on a trip, canceling a planned outing, going to the doctor, or being dropped off with friends or relatives should be brought up at the last minute to minimize a child's anxiety. Not so. Telling a child in advance of something important also tells him you believe he can make the adjustment. It is a long-term parenting philosophy.

THE THREE-DAY METHOD

When considering a transition from the bottle to a cup, think in terms of a countdown. I suggest that you give your child three days' notice before starting the process of taking away his bottle. If all goes according to plan, soon your child will be bottle free! As you prepare yourself for this seemingly daunting task, your attitude must be calm and casual. You want to instill in your child the confidence that you have that he will be okay without his bottle. Just as important, you want to continue to remind yourself about the likely tirade to follow. Be unrelenting. You will get through it.

When you first tell your child the news that his bottle days are coming to an end, in all likelihood he will not react with the ferocious resistance you might expect. The reason is quite simple: in your child's mind, this plan is a long way off!

Finally, choose a time to talk with your child when he is feeling relaxed and pleased with himself. Be sure you do not pick a time when he is tired or going to bed, or when he is parked in front of the television with the bottle in his mouth.

The bottle habit is not such a painful habit to break; more painful is the parent having to endure the child's crying and whining. Although it can appear that taking the bottle away will be traumatic for your child, I can assure you it is not. The entire process is totally dependent on your reaction and your leadership. You must be sure you build his confidence that he can do without it. Never let him feel with your soothing tone that he is falling apart and can't handle being without his bottle. Never say, "Poor little boy," or use platitudes like, "There, there Michael, it will be better," or belittling expressions such as "Cut it out, you're acting like a baby." Give him confidence and encouragement through your facial expressions and words. Use expressions like "I know this is hard. I know you can do this." These are not magic words that will make all the whining go away, they are words to make the helpless feelings go away. You must repeat and repeat and repeat, but it will work!

This little talk you have with your toddler is not a lecture. Lectures raise anxiety levels and produce glazed-over eyes. Your talk should not last more than thirty seconds. I call it the thirty-second rule. If you can't say it clearly in thirty seconds, don't say it! Collect your thoughts, and rehearse until you can say it all in thirty seconds. Parents generally go into far too much detail with lessons, lectures, and over-the-top stories with their children. Be succinct. Your thirty-second description of the plan should sound like casual information about what's to come.

In fact, the thirty-second rule applies to most communication where the news may be positive or negative: "Daniel, next week I have to go to a business meeting. I will be in San Diego. I'll be back in two days." Your tone and facial expression are calm and informal. The key is not to make a moment into an event! Whatever follow-up questions your child asks, remain calm and answer the questions with a reassuring smile. The underlying principle for this method, maintaining a calm directness, is something you will want to use throughout these parent-guidance years. Talking in a direct way shows respect— no tricking, no distractions, no elaborate, apologetic made-up stories. This should not mean your emotions are flat. A caring tone is *always* front and center.

The length of time it takes for your child to accept what you say is largely dependent on your style of communicating. "Talking up" to a child really means talking *with* him. It means not talking down to him, not talking at him, and not ignoring what he is saying. Actually speaking with your child is talking with a genuine faith that your child knows you believe in him and that he can do it! Talking up to a child will feel more relaxed and natural for you as well, and is *less* taxing. It takes more energy to talk down to your child than it does to talk *with* him.

The next step is to stop any baby talk: "Lilly, where's your pacie?"; "Does Bobby Boo want more ba ba?" Some parents add the suffix *y* to their child's first name: "Good boy, Mikey"; "Put it here, Greggy." Many parents actually call their toddlers by the name Baby instead of their real names: "Baby, do you want something to eat?" Although this may sound cute and loving to the parent, the toddler hears it differently. For a toddler, baby talk reinforces the feeling that he or she is still an infant.

The toddler will mimic the baby talk instead of learning real words, which conflicts with her own natural maturity and need for autonomy. This is a time for rapid vocabulary expansion: although the toddler's speaking vocabulary may be limited, her listening vocabulary is extensive! If baby talk continues into the toddler years, behavioral maturity will almost always be delayed.

Give him confidence and encouragement through your facial expressions and words. Use expressions like "I know this is hard. I know you can do this."

Day One

Prescription

Twice a day/30 seconds each morning and bedtime

When you find the right moment, in a *slow* manner say, "Alex, I would like to tell you something. I can see how you want to do a lot of things that make you older. That's a good idea. I can see you're ready to start. In three days it will be time to say good-bye to *all* your bottles. In three days it will be time to stop using all of them. I know you understand. We will do this together." Wait for his reaction, and *if* there is one, whatever he says, reflect it back. That's it. The whole talk should take thirty seconds. Do not give any impression that you are seeking his approval or permission. Use the same delivery as you would if you were telling him about an upcoming trip to the park. Typically, you will get back just a nod or a certain look that lets you know he got the message. You should talk in a way that shows you have confidence in him to make this work. Do not make the moment into an event! Later that night when he asks for his bottle, remind him again about your earlier talk. "Alex, remember our talk this morning about giving up the bottle. I can really see how you want to do a lot of things that make you older. That's a good idea. I can see you're ready to start. In three days it will be time to say good-bye to *all* your bottles. In three days it will be time to stop using all of them. I know you understand. We will do this together." Wait for his reaction, and *if* there is one, whatever he says, reflect it back. That's it. Then along with your normal routine, if he asks for his bottle, give it to him. That was day one. So far, so good!

Day Two

Prescription:
Twice a day/30 seconds each morning and bedtime

Day two should be essentially a repeat of day one. Whatever fuss he may make, stay with your message and just reflect his feelings as you continue with your plan. Do not sell him on the idea; it will only challenge and anger him more. Do not engage him or be drawn into any long conversations. The key is few words and more reflection.

That was day two.

Day Three

As this is the day you are physically going to gather up all his bottles, you will want to make sure you have put aside about twenty to thirty minutes. You can do this either in the morning or afternoon. Begin by telling him directly and calmly, "Alex, today is the third day. It is time to gather up all your bottles." If you have read him *Bottle Bowling!* remind him of the story. Use the concept of self-talk (a kind of thinking out loud): "Mmmmm, I wonder how many rooms they are in?" To be fair, he really won't be able to supply the answer, but you can be sure he understands the question and what will happen. It will be another reminder about the talk you had a few days ago, and it will help make him become a more active partner. If he does complain, which in all likelihod he will, continue to reflect back with a strong sense of empathy your understanding that he does not want to do this: "Alex, you don't feel like stopping the bottle now." Do not engage in any selling of the idea or talking about how much older he will feel without it. You must maintain a quiet and relaxed confidence both in yourself and him that he can go through this. "Alex, you can do this. I know you understand. You're ready now." Talk in fifteen-second sound bites—that's it. Let him watch you go from room to room finding his bottles. It should be done in a relaxed way, *not* punitively. Think of it in terms of casually going into his room and picking up his clothes and toys, which you probably do anyway. Be sure to reflect whatever feelings he is expressing, but *be unwavering about sticking to the plan.*

As you walk around finding each bottle, place them one by one into a plastic bag. Try to enlist your child's help, but if he does not want to help, that's okay too. Keep going. Don't forget to also include looking in the backseat of your car or SUV. As you do this, the energy may change with the fun feeling that you are on a scavenger hunt. Keep the momentum going with commentary like "Mmmm, I wonder how many we'll find in our car?" Do not do a lot of talking. Assuming your child has been watching you do this, let him see you place the bottles one at a time into the plastic bag. It would be even more effective if your child actually places some of them in the bag with you. This will mark a turning point, as he sees this is for real. Remind him: "Remember our talk about the three days?" During this exchange, be sure *not* to sound like you're asking for permission to do this. If your child is having a crying tantrum, say "You don't like that I remembered the three days. You wish I had forgotten. You wish there was more time left."

As you finish placing the last bottle into the bag, tell him that you will be sending them to a special place called a recycling center. That is where plastics and rubber are kept to make other things, like toys, plastic plates, and even parts for cars. Then walk to the front door of your house or apartment and leave the bag outside. Tell him you are leaving them by the door because someone will pick them up. (Obviously, that someone is you.) Use the next minute or so to explain about the recycling process and the special machinery involved in pounding and pulverizing. Also let your child know that when you pass a recycling drop-off center on the road (at supermarkets, etc.), you will be sure to point one out for him to see. This conversation, while upsetting to him, is also calming because of the interesting new information and details he is acquiring. He may look or act like he is tuning out, but he is tuning in. Remember, your child's listening vocabulary is at least fifty times greater than his speaking vocabulary. Many parents in the middle of this plan just dump the bottles in the garbage. I do not recommend that. You will get much more mileage out of the recycling story for days and weeks ahead than letting your child see them dumped into the garbage can.

Within a few minutes, when your child is out of sight, you should retrieve the bag of bottles and really put them in the recycling bin at your house or apartment. If you do have the time and patience, and really want to complete the process impeccably, put your child in the car and drive together to a recycling drop-off center. At the same time, if it is not possible or practical, just throw them away.

That's it.

I can assure you that within forty-eight hours or *less* your child will be finished with the bottle habit. Try not to cave in by keeping one bottle in reserve. This plan will work! As with pulling off a Band-Aid, the slower you pull, the more pain. Don't be surprised if during the next few months, as you pass a recycling drop-off center, he remarks, "Look—my babas are in there." Acknowledge this, and assure him that you remember. If your child wants his bottle back, don't be baited into a contest of wills: in a calm and patient way, just repeat the information about what you both knew would happen and did happen. Your child may well appear upset, but he will also feel safe in how you delivered a review of your plan.

Although the direct Three-Day Method is best, here are eight other quick ideas that can work too:

PLAY "PILLOW WISH"

Ask your child, "Do you sometimes wish for things? Me too. Sometimes they come true and sometimes they don't. Sometimes they can happen when we don't expect them. Zack, you know how sometimes you wish you didn't need your bottle? Well, tonight we'll play pillow wish." Then have the child place all his bottles under his pillow at night. (No need to be literal. Four or five will do.) Be sure he helps somewhat in locating them and placing them there. When he wakes up, the bottles are gone, replaced by a new toy or plaything he has been wanting. Be sure to tell your child in advance about the wishing game and be sure the chosen toy is a real surprise. When your child asks for his bottle back during moments of frustration, acknowledge his feelings, but remind him of the game: "You're missing your bottle—even though you are happy with your wish, sometimes that can happen."

SNIPPETY SNIP

Out of sight of your child, snip the end of the nipple off a bottle. Then before she asks for her bottle, show her how dangerous the rubber has become: "Look, Jessica—look at the rubber tip. That's called jagged. Can you say *jagged?* They sure can be dangerous and make the rubber taste funny." Explain that the damaged bottle is too dangerous to keep and the others are also a danger, even though they have not torn yet. Show a genuine concern and surprise. If possible, have the child herself throw the bottle in the trash can. If the child demands to be bought a new bottle, in a calm but reassuring tone tell her it's time to buy a cup and that she can pick it out. If she insists on wanting the bottle, accept that feeling, but repeat that it's time now for a cup. Don't personalize it by saying that it is time for *her specifically* to have a new cup. This can sound degrading and sets up a challenge. Be realistic; this will take many rounds. Be firm but understanding.

THE LIMIT RULE

Using limits to modify behavior has many variations. You could limit bottle use to certain rooms and keep decreasing the number of rooms in which use is allowed until there are none left. Begin by not allowing use anywhere but home. Or try a time limitation—let's say five minutes in certain rooms—or permit usage only at nap time and bedtime, and eventually only at bedtime.

THE FULL TUMMY/FULL SCHEDULE

It may seem obvious, but a tired or hungry child is more apt to feel insecure and be less equipped to deal well with stressful situations. Eat frequent, healthy meals, do projects, and engage in any physical activity that keeps the child's hands busy. The longer he goes, the less dependent he becomes. This is more tiring for the parent but it is also very effective.

THE CUP PRIZE

Play any simple game at home and let your child know that if she wins, she gets a prize—a new sippy cup! Take her to the store to buy it! Show what it looks like and leave it out each day so she can look at it or play with it. It will become more familiar as well as a motivating target when you talk about stopping with the bottle.

THE GRADUAL PHASE-OUT

This moderate approach can work but can also be a trap for frequent battles, so be prepared. It works best with younger toddlers over a period of about ten days or so.

- Decrease the number of bottles you offer during the day, replacing them with cups of warm milk or snacks.
- Water down the bottles of milk but serve undiluted milk in a cup.
- Phase out the midday bottle first.
- Try using a funny straw—it makes cups more fun.

THE SURPRISE

Offer your child a surprise, such as a snack that he loves, for making it through a day or night without his bottle. Be sure you do not offer toys or some other gift *before* he has done without it. Hint at a surprise only after the child has completed a day or so; it can be a snack or something that has a special meaning. Although effective, bribes are short-term fixes. As children get older, you will find bribes do not encourage natural motivation and insight. As the age increases, so does the price of bribery.

THE "LET IT BE" PLAN

Let him have the bottle for bedtime. Your bet is that sometime prior to his taking his SATs, he'll say, "Yeah, I guess I'm done!"

SEVEN

Thumb-Sucking

Tension and fear have a terrible effect on children, even though they may make children be still.

—JEANETTE GALAMBOS STONE

Starting the Thumb-Sucking Habit

When Karen saw her first ultrasound, she was looking for the obvious clues that would tell her whether she was going to have a boy or a girl. What she noticed instead was the outline of her infant with a thumb in its mouth. All healthy infants start life and sustain it with an urge to suck. This instinct is so strong that most newborns are not satisfied by feedings alone; they must continue to suck on something after their food needs are satisfied. If a baby becomes used to the thumb over a period of weeks or months, chances are good he will refuse the pacifier. He has learned to enjoy not only the sensations in his mouth but also the sensations on his thumb. Reasons vary, but by the time they become toddlers, most children discover thumb-sucking to be comforting when they are tired, afraid, hungry, or sleepy. Still, as many as 50 percent of newborns never try to thumb-suck at all or do it only casually and for brief periods. This should not be read into as any significant psychological sign at all. There is almost no evidence to suggest that kids who suck their thumbs are more troubled than those who do not. Known as the natural pacifier, thumb-sucking or finger-sucking can typically continue through the first three to five years. The pacifier, when introduced and used correctly, can prevent thumb-sucking: most infants who use a pacifier in the first three months of life never become thumb-suckers, even if they give up the pacifier at as early as four months.

Fifty years ago, thumb-sucking was considered a repulsive habit, ranking just above nail-biting. Pediatricians maintained that it was a sign of maladjustment and prescribed vinegar and bitters to be placed on the thumb. Some even went as far as to recommend keeping certain garments on the hands and appliances in the mouth to discourage the habit. Today, child-development professionals are less concerned with the long-term effects of thumb-sucking. A number of studies have found no relation between thumb-sucking and any later neuroses. In most cases, it is a form of self-soothing and nurturing that a child does in his pursuit of autonomy. However, the habit should not extend beyond four years of age and certainly should cease before the start of school and the arrival of permanent teeth. Both school and teeth can be negatively affected by continuing the thumb-sucking habit: the risk of both dental and social problems is great enough that the child must be helped to stop thumb-sucking. About 20 percent of five-year-olds suck their thumb and approximately 5 percent of children who are ten years old continue the habit. As a rule, more boys than girls become chronic thumb-suckers.

As with stopping the pacifier, many parents worry unnecessarily that the trauma caused by stopping thumb-sucking will be worse than the consequences. This is understandable, but untrue. If it were true, the child who quit thumb-sucking would immediately cling more strongly to other transitional objects and comforts, but as a rule, once thumb-sucking stops, that's it! With the exception of a child who has experienced a severe trauma, thumb-sucking becomes an empty habit.

Some observers have noted that thumb-suckers tend to be less responsive and tune out more of their environment when engaged in this behavior. In addition to shutting out the world, they tend to be made fun of more often at school, reminding them of this babylike behavior. A four- or five-year-old who still puts his thumb in his mouth is clearly engaged in a habit. A habit can be defined as an involuntary pattern of behavior. Other behaviors falling under this umbrella are bed-wetting, nail-biting, tics such as rapid eye-blinking, over-eating, and stuttering. All tend to be automatic reactions to anxiety.

Physical and Emotional Side Effects of Thumb-Sucking

Many parents ask if early substitution of a pacifier during infancy could be a preventative prescription for thumb-sucking. In some cases, yes. Babies who become regular thumb-suckers in their first three months may continue to be thumb-suckers for years. By contrast, most pacifier-suckers are ready to give up their habit much earlier, in most instances by two and a half years of age. Still, with the right help from Mom and Dad, both habits can be successfully broken.

If your child's thumb-sucking habit continues beyond the

time when permanent teeth start to appear, he may develop crooked teeth and a malformed palate. This results from pressure applied by the thumb on the teeth and roof of the mouth. The severity of the problem depends on the frequency, intensity, and duration of the thumb-sucking, as well as the position in which the thumb is placed in the mouth. The relationship between the upper and lower jaws may also be affected. Some research suggests that thumb-sucking typically exerts pressure upward on the palate, outward on the upper front teeth, and inward on the lower front teeth. This tends to make the upper front teeth protrude, the lower front teeth to tip in, and the palate to narrow. These three effects, termed malocclusion, are also referred to as buckteeth or open bite.

The longer the child persists in the habit beyond about age six, the greater the risk of permanent malocclusion. If it continues after a child begins losing his primary teeth, thumb-sucking can not only deform the bones of his young jaws but can also act like a crowbar to permanently unbalance the jaw muscles. Once unbalanced, these jaw muscles may keep distorting the jaws even more as he grows. Sometimes a crossbite occurs, with back teeth drawn in, as constant sucking narrows the palate. The trouble doesn't stop with teeth. Thumb-sucking can also lead to tongue-thrusting, which makes it difficult to pronounce consonants like *s, r, d, t, n, z,* and *l.* Many lisp until the thumb is given up. Speech defects can also occur as a result of malaligned teeth from prolonged thumb-sucking and/or finger-sucking. If the habit is stopped before the permanent teeth erupt, the problem can usually be reversed.

Although many children suck their thumb out of nervousness, anxiety, or boredom, it is a habit that can be, and should be, broken.

The emotional problems involved with thumb-sucking can be socially debilitating. Although many children suck their thumb out of nervousness, anxiety, or boredom, it is a habit that can be, and should be, broken. Far more than pacifiers or any other transitional object, the thumb is a constant physical and emotional reminder to the child that he is still a little boy. His thumb is almost always wet, smelly, and wrinkly, and because he always has it under his control, it becomes one of the most difficult habits to break. Emotional problems that are associated with thumb-suckers include low self-esteem, nervousness, and teasing from other children. Although many parents feel anxious about interfering with their child's ability to soothe himself, it is highly recommended that you help your child break his thumb-sucking habit well before he begins kindergarten. Schoolchildren can be unmerciful in class and in the school yard. They can be particularly mean to thumb-suckers. The best approach for parents to take is to explain to the child that the habit itself is causing the teasing, and not the child's personality. This way the peer pressure becomes a motivational factor for the child.

Emotional problems that are associated with thumb-sucker include low self-esteem, nervousness, and teasing from other children. Although many parents feel anxious about interfering with their child's ability to soothe himself, it is highly recommended that you help your child break his thumb-sucking habit well before he begins kindergarten.

That is why I tell parents that if they see their child at two years of age sucking his thumb, they should break the habit then.

One final thought: Don't pressure your child to quit during a high-stress time in his life. If other things have been going on that affect your child, such as a death, divorce, or moving, hold off until a more calm and peaceful time arrives. When you decide to start, pick a deadline for stopping. Have your child help you pick this date—but don't let him select one that is three years away! Maybe you want to keep track of how many days or hours the child goes without sticking his thumb in his mouth. Maybe you want to set up a system that involves the child recognizing his feelings and requires your ongoing encouragement every time he comes to you and says, "I feel ——, but I didn't suck my thumb." Reward behavior at a time when she least expects it. Be consistent: habits are hard to break.

How to Stop the Thumb-Sucking Habit

THE AROUND THE CLOCK METHOD

The *Around the Clock* method is the method of choice for helping a child to stop sucking his thumb. It works well for children ages four and up. Thumb-sucking is a much harder habit to break than the bottle or pacifier habit, so it will require a tremendous steadfast commitment on the part of the parent to help undo. For one thing, the thumb can't be taken away. Remind yourself to remain calm and *never, never* name-call, degrade, or compare your child to another sibling or schoolmate. Given the difficulties involved, just the thought of helping your child break this habit can make any parent want to delay the inevitable. As you prepare yourself for this new mission, remember to set and manage your expectations first. Be ready for this to take longer than you think: anywhere between days and three weeks. Prepare yourself for the full range of emotions and reactions your child will show. Anticipating what is ahead will decrease your stress level as well as your child's. And, finally, repeat to yourself, "I can do this"—because you can!

Before beginning this process, I highly recommend reading my children's storybook *Thumb Things to Do! Ideas You Never Knew.* It prepares your child in an honest and active way to stop her thumb-sucking habit. The story is packed with visual images and physical activity to help your child prepare for what she is about to do. It provides the child with a real sense of control. Read it once each day for five consecutive days before you start helping your child stop her habit. Reading *Thumb Things to Do!* will accelerate your child's success. You can find the book at www.parentfitness.com.

Effecting change in behavior is a dynamic process. While some behaviors are predictable, others are not. What may work well with one child may have to be slightly modified to work with another. However, the underlying principles of mutual respect and allowing for process go unchanged. So, before looking at the actual method, please take the time to read the context behind these ideas. Without adjusting your expectations and a full understanding of what you are about to do, these ideas will become just a cold set of techniques.

Just like an adult, a small child needs time to prepare for

change. I recommend giving a kind of heads-up, casual news flash with the information you want them to have. "Samantha, in three minutes we are leaving the house to go to the store. You can suck your thumb until then, but then you must stop. When we return, you can do it again. I know you can do this. You understand?" Asking that question at the end serves to bring the child into the moment. Children will adjust easier to new changes if you tell them in advance. This applies to most situations that involve a nagging anxiety about some future event. For bigger issues, like stopping the thumb-sucking habit, you should announce these changes to your child at least three to five days in advance of when it will start. For some reason, parents feel that talking about a future change of plans such as going away on a trip, canceling a planned outing, going to the doctor, or being dropped off with friends or relatives should be brought up at the last minute to minimize a child's anxiety. Not so. Telling a child in advance of something important also tells him you believe he can make the adjustment. It is a long-term parenting philosophy.

This philosophy of being direct is *not* a license to bark out orders or instructions. You want to be sure that you are not yelling and bullying your way when enforcing a rule you previously set.

If you're not expressing authentic empathy—"Aaron, I know you miss sucking your thumb, you wish you could do it now"—you will continue to undermine the trust between you and your child. Physically taking the child's thumb out of his mouth is the easy part. Your words are meaningless unless accompanied with a sincere tone and gesture.

In the case of ending the thumb-sucking habit, think in terms of a countdown. I suggest that you give your child three days to prepare *before* stopping his thumb-sucking. If all goes according to plan, your child will soon be thumb free! As you prepare yourself for this seemingly daunting task, your attitude must be calm and casual. You want to instill in your child the confidence that you have that he will be okay without his thumb. Just as important, you want to continue to remind yourself about the likely tirade to follow. Be unrelenting. You will get through it.

Here are the seven elements that help break the thumb-sucking habit:

- Have a Heads-Up Talk
- Talk with Respect
- Use Code Words for "Stop"
- Mark the Calendar
- Play Mirror, Mirror
- Keep Reminding
- Show Deep Belief in the Child

Have a Heads-Up Talk

In a relaxed way, let your child know what he intuitively already knows: his thumb-sucking must stop. Find the right time to have this little talk: when your child is feeling relaxed and his thumb is *not* in his mouth. Be direct, and let him know how easy it is for anyone to get into a habit. If your child is older than five, keep your talk to under one minute! Be careful not to excite anxiety with dramatic stories about how thumb-sucking will likely damage her life. Give her the information about habits in a matter-of-fact way, taking care not to make comparisons, such as "You're too big to be doing that" or "Your brother Bobby never sucked his thumb." Remember, ultimately it is up to your child to break the habit—you can not do it *for* her, but you can offer plenty of encouragement. Above all, your child has to feel a genuine belief from you that you really believe she can succeed at this. Do not underestimate this kind of communication. Faith in a child (like an adult) cannot be faked, even if the right words are spoken.

When you first tell your child the news that his thumb-sucking days are coming to an end, in all likelihood he will not react with the ferocious resistance you might expect. The reason is quite simple: in your child's mind, this plan is a long way off! Remember, the talk you have with your child should last no more than one minute. No lectures—lectures raise anxiety levels and produce glazed-over eyes. Your talk should start with a thirty-second sound bite. If you can't say it clearly in thirty seconds, don't say it! Collect your thoughts and rehearse until you can say it in thirty seconds. Parents go into way too much detail with lessons, lectures, and over-the-top stories. Be succinct. Your thirty-second statement should sound like casual information about what's to come. For example, you might want to say something like "Danielle, I know sometimes you don't want to put your thumb in your mouth. I know you want to control yourself and you can. We can practice stopping together." After waiting for her response, reassure her, "I know you can do this." If you have read her *Thumb Things to Do!* remind her of the story.

Calmly communicating news that is uncomfortable works very well in all situations. For example: "Danielle, next week I have to go out of town to a business meeting. I will be in San Diego. I'll be back in three days." Your tone and facial expression are calm and informal. The key is not to make a moment into an event! Whatever follow-up questions your child asks, remain calm and answer the questions with a reassuring smile. The underlying principle for remaining calm is something you will want to use throughout these parent-guidance years.

Talk with Respect

Talking in a direct way shows respect—no tricking, no distractions, no elaborate, apologetic made-up stories. This should not mean your emotions are flat. A caring tone is always front and center. The length of time it takes for your child to accept what you say is largely dependent on your style of communicating. Talking up to a child really means talking *with* him. It means not talking down to him, not talking at him, and not ignoring what he is saying. Talking up to a child will feel more relaxed and natural for you as well, and is *less* taxing. It takes more energy to talk down to your child than it does to talk *with* him.

Quitting the thumb-sucking habit does not have to be traumatic. You want to stress dialogue and respect. If you threaten, bully, or forbid the behavior, you will wage a battle you cannot win. Let your child know you are on her side by asking her to suggest some ways to practice so she can remember to catch herself when she goes for her thumb. Try to avoid using the word *help* as much as possible: on the face of it, the word *help* seems innocent enough, but it is a word that in all likelihood surrounds the child at home and in school. The word *help* is ubiquitous in her life. It totally undermines the child's well-being. Count how many times a day you use the word *help*. Add to that number the number of times your child hears that word from teachers, extended family, and other people every day. So many offers of help can make a child feel helpless and incapable of accomplishing anything on her own. Instead, use the word *practice* rather than *help,* as it makes the point in a more effective way. So rather than asking your child how you can help her, ask her for some ways the two of you can practice together so she will not suck her thumb. Including her in generating ideas is critical even if you come up with all the ideas. *Practice* is active and gives her some control, and what's more, it's something everyone does. Remind her that everyone practices, even our favorite athletes and musicians. Parents should be quick to include themselves when talking with their children about this daily process too: "David, I'm going to go to my office today to practice doing a better job in writing those reports. They're due on Wednesday."

> **Try to avoid using the word *help* as much as possible: on the face of it, the word *help* seems innocent enough, but it is a word that in all likelihood surrounds the child at home and in school. The word *help* is ubiquitous in her life. It totally undermines the child's well-being.**

Use Code Words for "Stop"

Children do not respond well to lectures, or a constancy in hearing you say stop. By the age of five you can be sure they fully feel their own problems and don't need a lecture to make a point more clear. In that regard, make up a word that you and your child agree on, so that when you are in public, all you do is say that word to remind your child that he has his thumb in his mouth. Words like *skateboard, goozad,* or *zoo* will work just fine. Be sure it is a word chosen by your child and *not* you. Such shorthand saves time and embarrassment.

Mark the Calendar

Marking the days off the calendar can provide a dramatic reminder for your child of his progress, and it can be a springboard from which to initiate further growth. For instance, you might recall for him the days when he sucked his thumb all day and congratulate him on now having learned to get through the night thumbless too. Then go to the calendar: "Let's mark off how many days left before we completely stop—look, nine more days. I know you can do this." If you take this approach, be prepared for some restless days and nights. The thumb-sucking habit is a hard one to break. Be sure you reflect whatever feelings he is expressing, but *be unwavering about sticking to the plan.*

Play Mirror, Mirror

Part of your practicing to stop the habit (let your child hear you refer to thumb-sucking as a habit) is to stand him (his thumb in his mouth) in front of the mirror, two or three times a day, for about three minutes each stretch. Your child may resist at first, but gradually he will get used to it. Ask him to notice details about his face, hand, or fingers, or the expressions he makes when his thumb is inside his mouth. By timing him, you are calling attention to this as an exercise. Most children are not used to seeing themselves and what they look like. It is very effective. Let your child lead in this exercise, while you reflect back and give confidence and encouragement: "You noticed the way your thumb bends and how the saliva drips down. I can see you really want to stop this habit, you notice it hides your face. Soon it will be over." Keep all of the dialogue on the level of observation, not interpretation. Be sure not to ask the child how it makes him feel.

Keep Reminding

Do not be shy about reminding your child each and every time he is sucking his thumb. Also, do not hesitate to put your hand on his hand and remove the thumb from his mouth. Also remind him that quitting, like anything else new he wants to do, takes practice, and acknowledge his effort: "You've been practicing hard. I can see that."

It is worth repeating: avoid lecturing and using the word *help*. Think about yourself at work or in any other situation where you want to prove yourself. If thirty or forty times a day you heard, "Fred, need some help, want some help, you look like you can use some help, let me know when you want some help," these statements would reinforce feelings of real help-lessness. Use the word *practice* instead of *help*. Applying this new word can have a positive and powerful effect on your child's self-esteem if practiced diligently. The immediate feeling created is one of getting ahead and getting the edge, because practice gives the child an active incentive.

Show Deep Belief in the Child

One of the most important gifts a parent can give a child is to show a consistent *deep belief* in him. It applies not just to breaking a certain habit, but in building the good habits you want him to practice. Your child will know whether you *really* believe in him, or whether you just *say* you do. During the time you are practicing with your child to conquer his fears and habits, there will be many setbacks. Your job is not to draw attention to that fact, but to keep building on your child's positive attitude about stopping. Any hesitation or frustration on your part, anything that could signal to the child that *you* are frustrated, will indicate that you really do not believe in him. *It will be your authentic belief in him that will provide the confidence for him to believe in himself.* If during the process of breaking habits too much pressure is put on your child, or if he is made to feel bad, he may retaliate by not quitting.

It will be your authentic belief in the child that will provide the confidence for him to believe in himself.

Here are two additional ideas that might prove useful in breaking the thumb-sucking habit:

- Help find your child another transitional object as a replacement for her thumb.
- A mild deterrent, such as a bitter taste on the thumb, can turn an unconscious habit into a conscious one.

EIGHT

Bears, Blankets, and Everything Else!

The smaller the person, the less we worry about his dignity. Sometimes we even find the idea a little ludicrous, as if smallness and inexperience were incompatible with anything so majestic as human dignity. . . . Yet children have a great sense of their own dignity. They couldn't define what it is but they know when it has been violated.

—LEONTINE YOUNG, SOCIAL WORKER

Choosing a Bear or Blanket

Children's catalogs are big business. Collector-edition bears, dolls, robots, licensed toy characters, and everything in between . . . all offer children a chance to take home a newfound friend. What makes these characters so appealing? In large part, a toy's appeal is that it allows a child's expression of his basic drive to relate to and control something apart from himself. The transitional object helps bridge events through the divides of life. The teddy bear, perhaps our best-known transitional pal, follows many children to bed to ease the transition from togetherness to aloneness, from waking to sleeping, and from lightness to darkness.

During one of my Parent Fitness Training workshops, a couple going through a high-conflict marital impasse told of how they'd noticed that their five-year-old daughter was becoming far more attached than usual to her mother's side. It was obvious that their fighting was leaving their daughter feeling more insecure about her place in the family. It was also obvious that they both needed to immediately stop competing to be the "good one" versus the "bad one" in the eyes of their daughter. Doing so puts the child in the untenable position of choosing a side and is emotionally disastrous for her. Even when one spouse is clearly the offender, careful self-control on the part of the healthier parent is required to not put the other parent in a bad light. Although this is difficult to do, it is crucial. In an effort to help stave off some of the anxiety their daughter was feeling about their conflict, I recommended a trip to the store together to select a brand new little stuffed animal. By being present at the time of selection, the mother and father add their own special qualities to the experience and the object. As such, the transitional object has a memory of each parent within it, becoming a fantasy symbol of harmony. The result: when the child retreats to play with or hold that object, the child can feel an increased level of security from Mom and Dad.

> The teddy bear, perhaps our best-known transitional pal, follows many children to bed to ease the transition from togetherness to aloneness, from waking to sleeping, and from lightness to darkness.

Early Attachments

The idea of introducing a transitional object at around ten months of age is a good one. You can begin by putting different things in your child's crib or holding him at the same time he holds a blanket or soft toy. Be sure as you put him down for the night you put his little object with him. Try not to force a selection, as not all infants will show interest in just one object. As your baby nears his eleventh month, an attachment should

have begun to form. Stay with that same object. One sugges-
tion: if you decide to introduce a small blanket, try those soft
white cloth diapers. They're easy to clean and your child will
not be able to tell one from the other. For practical reasons,
such as not having to scour the house when the diaper/
blanket gets misplaced, this works great.

Whatever the child's chosen object, many months later it
will serve as a powerful reminder of how she was held by you.
Children use their transitional objects in an infinite number of
ways and at the most unexpected times. If you watch closely,
you can see them interact with their chosen object when they
are overtired and cranky, or perhaps when they've unexpect-
edly hurt themselves. When they get older and begin day care,
many children have trouble separating from one or both parents. Under these circumstances, it is a good idea for the parent
to encourage the child to take his object with him to the day
care center. Practically speaking, then, it's a good idea for the
attachment object to be an item that's easy to carry around.
Some day care centers may not allow your child to bring along
personal objects from home. In such a case, parents should explain the day care's rules to the child, but allow him to bring
his transitional object with him in the car.

Many psychologists have suggested that the characteristics
of our first attachments influence all of our later attachments
and our overall emotional and social development. Generally
speaking, children who have experienced a "secure" attachment style with their parents, generally will have the easiest
time with relationships. However, whatever attachment style

your child has now was probably determined during the first three years of life.

In the 1960s and 1970s, the child psychologist Mary Ainsworth theorized that all attachments were not the same, but could be divided into three broad categories: secure, anxious/ambivalent, and avoidant. She based her conclusions on twelve-month-old infants observed in "strange and new situations." In this experiment, mothers brought their children to a room with a stranger and the child's special toys. The mothers soon left, leaving their children with the stranger. After a short while, they returned, then left, and returned again. Each time the mother returned, Ainsworth observed the infant's behavior, using it to classify the baby's attachment style. Securely attached infants were happy to see their mothers return. Typically, they clung to their mothers for a while, then turned to play with their special toys. Anxious/ambivalent infants initially appeared happy to see their mothers return, but often quickly became angry and some tried pushing them away. They were not truly comforted by their mothers' return. Avoidant infants appeared indifferent to their mothers' return.

What we learn from these studies is that toddlers and young children gain enormous benefits through their familiar transitional toy objects in resolving conflicts they are feeling. Knowing this, we must be careful not to degrade a child's attachments with such statements as "Only babies use a blankie" or "Big boys don't need a teddy bear!" Not only are these statements untrue, but they serve only to humiliate and undermine a critical part of a child's development. Among the most common reasons for reliance on transitional objects are the feelings of separation and abandonment. Sometimes Mom or Dad is *not* available, and the transitional object is an important connection to him or her. These early fears of abandonment, and the need for transitional objects, continue right through the middle childhood years.

In 1997, as reported by the American Psychological Association, three-year-olds from sixty-four families were observed to see if security blankets aided in reducing stress during routine medical examinations. After asking parents to identify their child as attached or not attached to a security blanket, each child, at random, was assigned to one of the following scenarios during an examination: mother only, security blanket only, mother and security blanket, or neither mother nor blanket. Measurements of heart rate and blood pressure during the exam were noted, as was the observed level of distress. Findings showed that children identified as attached to a security blanket or bear who were allowed to keep their blanket during the exam demonstrated considerably less distress.

Stuffed Animal Safety

Although it is far less common than other safety issues, there are unfortunately some risks involved in playing with certain stuffed animals. In any given year, the U.S. Consumer Product Safety Commission (CPSC) in Washington sends out alerts for hundreds of product recalls for items that may pose hazards to children. Both well-known companies as well as small start-ups are included in these alerts. Some of the problems have been related to the noses, bells, and eyes of the stuffed animals, as well as buttons and other accessories that can detach and pose a choking hazard to young children. The eyes in particular can present a sharp-point hazard. Make sure these parts are attached properly and securely. Parents who have allergy-prone children must also be on the lookout for stuffed animals that may shed easily. Reading labels is mandatory, as stuffed animals may present a risk for any number of adverse skin reactions and rashes.

The U.S. Consumer Product Safety Commission protects the public from unreasonable risks of injury or death from fifteen thousand types of consumer products under the agency's jurisdiction. According to the CPSC, one company, in February 2002, recalled nearly 3.9 million plush teddy bears because of potential choking hazards after receiving thirty-two reports of the toy's eyes and nose coming off. The company received three reports of children placing these small parts in their mouths. To report a dangerous product or a product-related injury, you can call CPSC's hotline at (800) 638-2772 or send a fax at (800) 638-8270. To order a list of recalls for problem products through fax-on-demand, call (301) 504-0051, or even better, log on to www.cpsc.gov/talk.html.

Emotional Overattachments

DON'T INTERFERE

With regard to children's transitional objects, the general rule is that unless your child is obsessed with his little bear friend, doll, action figure, or blanket, don't interfere. By this point in the book, you now know the power of such objects in the development of a child's inner world. To this day I've never seen a women walking down the aisle about to take her wedding vows toting her little blankie. A Hermès scarf, perhaps, but never a blankie. With rare exceptions, there is little value in forcing a child to give up the favorite object that over the years has held so many important memories. However, if she begins to trade in her outside activity and friends in order to be around her favorite stuffed animal, well, then it's time to both seek professional help and substantially limit the object's use.

> **With rare exceptions, there is little value in forcing a child to give up the favorite object that over the years has held so many important memories.**

We all remember from personal experience how brutal young children can be when they decide to make fun of another child's behavior. Carrying around a favorite stuffed animal when other children are not can be pretty humiliating for an older child. It may not be long before that child decides it's safer to stay indoors than venture outside and endure the slings and arrows of peers. The simple condition or appearance of a doll, bear, or blanket also plays a role in the reactions of others. It can look pretty nasty after a while, which can elicit unwanted attention and insults. Parents typically feel embarrassed and worry about why their child continues to need that dirty blanket or bear in the first place. Of course, such admonitions and judgments will only reinforce the child's dependence. Regardless of the poor condition, if you want to wash the child's little object to be more hygenic, always ask first if it is okay and respect his answer if you get back a resounding no.

Many parents are more embarrassed than disturbed when their child is found dragging her favorite blanket or stuffed animal from place to place in public. This misplaced embarrassment is best ignored. At the same time, though, for those who worry too much about certain behavior habits, we must ask the right questions in the context of the child's attachment before *prematurely* looking for her first therapist. Is she eating and sleeping well? Is she reasonably well behaved at home and in school? Does she have a regular group of playmates and friends? Does she prefer to be alone or around other children? Does she seem happy and secure most of the time? Does she play with kids her own age? If most of the answers to these questions aren't raising concerns, then it's a good bet that the blanket or stuffed animal is *not* a sign of any deep upset.

If your child is starting school, his object can also be a problem if the school has a policy against children bringing such items to school. In such cases, I suggest parents explain ahead of time to the teacher that their child, at this particular time, gets a great deal of comfort from his little bear. Let the teacher know that it may be temporary and how much you would appreciate it if he or she would help your child through this new phase of adjustment. Also add that as a bonus, the little object will help your child take naps more easily and keep him calmer in general and less susceptible to tantrums.

When your child is older and still insists on carrying her doll everywhere, you would be wise to listen closely to her reactions in new environments. She may be looking to you for the signal that she is ready to give up her attachment. At the same time, parents should also be aware that some situations may trigger an increased need for a security blanket. In our culture, research suggests that fathers express more negative attitudes toward boys who use security blankets or soft toys as transitional objects as opposed to little girls who use the same blankets or soft toys. As a rule, mothers usually express more positive attitudes toward all children who use such objects. For example, often when there is a change like a new baby, a move to a new house, or even a return from vacation, you might notice that your child has gone back to his teddy bear or blanket for extra comfort. While having a transitional object is a definite advantage for children, it does bring with it the burdens of remembering to carry it with them and being careful not to lose it. Many parents report that forgetting or losing a chosen object can trigger a meltdown. There is something fundamentally human about the need to feel safe or attach to something greater than ourselves when we are in fear of being alone. Even in the movie *Castaway,* we see a man marooned on an island create his own transitional object—a volleyball with a painted face—to help ease the pain of loneliness. Still, some children will reach a stage where they are ready to put them aside, only to have their development unwittingly undermined. For example, four-year-old Billy was happily playing in the living room at a friend's house with four or five other children while his mom was in the kitchen talking with her friends. Suddenly his mom said, "Oh, I forgot Billy's beanie rabbit in the car. I know he will miss it!" When she came into the living room to give it to him, Billy was embarrassed and reminded of his infantile behavior in front of his friends.

> There is something fundamentally human about the need to feel safe or attach to something greater than ourselves when we are in fear of being alone.

Parents who think that their five-year-old may be too attached to a favorite bear, doll, or action figure may be better served by examining the child's degree of attachment first. Does she prefer dolls to people? Does he prefer Buzz Lightyear to visiting friends? Probably not. The truth is, some parents may actually feel threatened that their child's relationship with his favorite bear or doll may at certain times offer more comfort than their own presence. Seven-year-old Daniel, for instance, returning home after being pushed down by an older boy at school, retreated to his room in search of his Woody cowboy figure from the movie *Toy Story*. His mom couldn't understand why he didn't want to be with her when he got home. That night, when she was putting him to bed, Daniel, while holding his cowboy figure, told her what had happened earlier at the park. This wise mother could see that he was working something out in his own mind and commented gently, "I see how much that bothered you." That comment led him to add, "I coulda pushed him back if I wanted to!" As she left the room, the mother turned and quietly said, "Yes, I can see you knew what to do." This open-ended empowering remark left Daniel with a sense of power and respect.

The ways in which children use their transitional objects tell us a great deal about their development. Unlike the thumb or pacifier, a stuffed animal or favorite toy can take on an unlimited number of play themes. As an alert parent, you will likely hear the child playing the role of *everyone* in and out of his family system—Mom, Dad, brothers, sisters, teachers, pets will all get their turn. You don't need to be a child psychologist to read into this: a good listening heart reveals how the child feels about certain people and places.

> **Unlike the thumb or pacifier, a stuffed animal or favorite toy can take on an unlimited number of play themes.**

Although most children will use transitional objects in play, children's needs differ when it comes to these objects. Some children never even have a true security object, but instead jump from one object to another for short periods of time; others cling to one object for years. As long as the relationship doesn't inhibit the child's development of social or language skills, there's no reason to be concerned. Transitional objects help the child deal with independence; they are considered to be experimental steps toward growing up. It's a big world out there, and anything within reason that gives a child comfort and solace is good. Parents may not always comprehend the importance of the object attachment for the child; a particular object usually has unique features that make it valuable to the child. However, a child unable to use an object for self-comfort and who instead becomes very withdrawn, or falls apart emotionally, will show a sign of distress. Of course, the best remedy for this will always be your own relationship and reflecting back what he is feeling or doing to help calm him down. In fantasy play, children interact with their stuffed animals and toys as they pretend to establish new relationships and experiences and rehearse personal skills and solutions.

FETISHES

Far rarer than the typical attachments to transitional objects are the more disturbing behaviors that develop when an attachment takes on an element of sexuality. These are called fetishes. The evolvement of fetishism and the selection of a particular fetish object can be quite complex. Even in the young child, the fetish has its precursors. Freud believed that the object was a substitution for a part of the body for sexual release. Evidence points to the cause of fetishism as a disturbed relationship with the mother. Fetishes are almost always related to sexual purposes, with the anxiety being discharged to some degree with the conclusion of certain activities or behaviors. This behavior is always marked by a certain degree of obsessiveness. For example, you may see a child habitually rubbing himself with his object, mounting it, licking it, and so forth. Early learning models suggest that a child who is the victim or observer of inappropriate sexual behaviors often learns to imitate the behavior and later is reinforced for such behavior. Such disturbing behaviors, as embarrassing as they may be, must *always* be brought to the attention of your pediatrician and ultimately, perhaps a play therapist.

The History of the Teddy Bear

The roots of the teddy bear cultural phenomenon are really quite amazing. Here's a snapshot ancestry of those *bear* facts!

These ubiquitous transitional objects found in the hands of millions of children actually began and continue to be in the hands of adults as well! The teddy bear made its appearance in America in late 1902, according to tradition, getting its start in a cartoon. Drawn by Clifford Berryman and titled "Drawing the Line in Mississippi," the cartoon showed President Theodore Roosevelt refusing to shoot a baby bear. According to this often-told tale, Roosevelt was on a hunting trip, but the hunting was so poor that someone finally captured a bear and invited Roosevelt to shoot it. Roosevelt's refusal to fire at such a helpless target inspired Berryman to draw his cartoon, which was published in *The Washington Post* on November 16, 1902. It caused an immediate sensation and was reprinted widely. Inspired by the cartoon, Morris and Rose Michtom of Brooklyn, New York, made a stuffed bear in honor of the president's actions. The Michtoms named their bear "Teddy's Bear" and placed it in the window of their candy and stationery store. Instead of looking fierce and standing on all four paws like previous toy bears, the Michtoms' bear looked sweet and innocent, and stood upright, like the bear shown in Berryman's cartoon. In fact, the demand was so strong that the Michtoms, with the help of a wholesale firm called Butler Brothers, founded the first teddy bear manufacturer in the United States, the Ideal Novelty and Toy Company.

The outbreak of World War II in Europe in 1939 stopped the momentum. Instead of making teddy bears, the world's workers and factories turned to the war effort. Some companies closed and never reopened. Strangely enough, the comeback of the teddy after years of mass production was triggered not by a bear maker, but by an actor. On television in the 1970s, British actor Peter Bull openly expressed his love for teddy bears and his belief in the teddy bear's importance in the emotional life of adults. He wrote a classic book entitled *Bear with Me* to celebrate the impact that teddy bears have on people's lives. As a result, he was invited to make radio and television appearances, including the *Tonight Show* with Johnny Carson. Without intending to, Bull created an ideal climate for the teddy bear to regain its popularity, not only as a children's toy, but as a collectible for adults.*

*From *Teddy Bear and Friends,* www.teddybearandfriends.com.

NINE

Television and the Internet

The most important factors in the life of their children
are not the school, the television set, the playmates, or the
neighborhood, but what the parents cherish,
what they hate, and what they fear.

—THOMAS HORA

The Ultimate Pacifier

The typical excuses parents offer when explaining why it is so difficult to limit children's television watching or Internet use are: "It's the only way I get any time for peace and quiet"; "Without TV, I can't get my housework done"; "My children get bored quickly doing other activities." Putting aside for the moment the body of evidence about the deleterious effects of too much television on a child's nervous system, television still remains the grandaddy of all pacifiers. What makes it even worse is the unwitting message parents give their children when they send them off to watch TV, play their videos, or log on to the Internet. Whether the child turns on the television by himself or the parent prepares the child with loving-kindness by setting him up with a pillow, a peanut butter and jelly sandwich, and juice makes no difference. The message is still the same: "I have no time or patience to be with you." With the pressures and exhaustion a parent faces today, it's easy to understand how the TV and Internet became the greatest secret pacifiers of our time. I say *secret* because we dare not admit how many hours we allow our children to indulge in them. A screaming toddler can almost always be quieted by watching the flicker of the tube. The problem with giving in to the TV demand, however, is that it removes the opportunity for the child to practice calming himself down. As nerve-racking as it is to listen to a screaming child ask for his favorite cartoon show, giving in and turning on the TV reinforces the message that you have no confidence in him to control himself. In turn, the child soon thinks: "Why should I stop myself? My mother or father will give in and turn on the TV."

When it comes time to enforce new time-limit rules about television watching, respect must still be the order of the day. Thinking first about how to say something, as opposed to just impulsively saying it, makes a vast difference: "Jonathan, in five minutes the TV will be turned off for the day," as opposed to walking in and clicking off the television. This may sound obvious, but it bears repeating because, since tensions run so high in families today and patience seems to be hitting a new low, parents find it harder and harder to speak to their children with calm respect. Part of the problem is the change in the American family system. A major element of this change can be seen in television programming where children *dis* (as in *disrespect*) their parents on a regular basis in these sitcoms. We've gone from watching *Father Knows Best* (and he did) to watching *The Simpsons,* where children have learned that Father knows nothing! An important antidote for such behavior is not allowing disrespect to flow on either side in the first place. Parents must be diligent in two ways. First, disrespectful backtalk must always be confronted. Never allow a child, either through body language or words, to show disrespect. Of course, a parent must model the same respect. There is a difference between accepting a child's feelings and accepting his behavior. Bad feelings are always tolerated; bad behavior is not! The second part of a parent's diligence is not allowing even two seconds of watching television shows that are complete garbage—no matter how popular.

Television Can Be Positive

Although this chapter makes clear the dangers of too much, as well as unsupervised, television watching and Internet access, it would be unfair not to present at least some of the benefits of supervised TV viewing or surfing. Clearly, television can be a positive force. It can stimulate imagination, so long as the child does not depend on it for imaginative activity, and it can help counter racial stereotypes. Television can also model and teach prosocial behavior, by moving extraordinary numbers of people to act charitably or unite. Studies have demonstrated that television can lead to increased generosity, cooperation, adherence to rules, delay of gratification, friendliness, and decreased fear. One show above all others has led that charge. The prosocial skills that the late, great Fred Rogers wrote into his scripts for *Mister Rogers' Neighborhood* stressed helping, sharing, delaying gratification, persisting, engaging in creative and imaginative play, and understanding others' points of view. Exposure of preschoolers to *Mister Rogers' Neighborhood* increased positive reinforcement of those social skills. We sure miss you, Mr. Rogers!

The real goal is to get your child not to think of the TV set as a pacifier but to see it as a source for collecting information. This is not easy, but it can be done. Empowering your child and encouraging him while watching can be worthwhile. Still, in the end, television watching is best when kept to a bare minimum. And what is the bare minimum? Less than three hours per week, total!

The Internet too, like television, has its positive forces. No one would deny the miracle of instant access to information, news, and knowledge from anywhere across the world. Saying it is anything less than *amazing* is not to recognize the *remarkable* tool the Internet can be for child and adult alike.

Emotional and Developmental Effects

However, too much television viewing can interfere with the development of thinking skills and imagination. A crucial element of thinking is extrapolating from what you know to figure out how it applies in a new situation. School requires this, television does not. Children who learn from typical television shows, show lower-than-normal expectations about the amount of mental effort required to learn from written texts, and tend to read less and perform relatively poorly in school. It takes very little mental effort to follow a TV show. Children raised on television believe it takes less effort to learn from books because they are used to being spoon-fed information by television characters.

Television's persistent sound and rapidly changing images can condition a child to expect a similar level of stimulation to be present almost everywhere, including at school and during general conversation. In school, a child will be called upon to speak, listen to a teacher, or read, none of which involves the attention-grabbing effect of television's dual stimuli. Anecdotal information from the college level suggests that one of the main reasons professors introduce multimedia (sound and image) segments into lectures is to retain the attention of television-raised students. A chalk-on-the-blackboard lecture leaves many students unable to remain attentive.

> **Television's persistent sound and rapidly changing images can condition a child to expect a similar level of stimulation almost everywhere, including at school and during general conversation.**

Conditioning a child to the short time periods of television is also an unintended by-product. The approximately seven-minute length of a typical program before a commercial interruption can condition a child to a seven-minute attention span. *The Wall Street Journal,* on February 10, 1994, related the experience of a professional storyteller, who performs before some ten thousand people a year, most of them children: after about seven minutes, he said, restlessness sets in as the children's inner clocks anticipate a commercial break. Schools expect kindergarteners through second-graders to have short attention spans, but also expect attention capability to increase with grade level. When that doesn't happen, children are disadvantaged.

Young marathon television viewers are missing more than good fun too, according to psychologist Dorothy G. Singer, Ph.D., codirector of the Yale University Family Television Research and Consultation Center. Make-believe, she says, teaches children such real-world skills as flexibility, empathy, and proficiency in planning. Consider, for instance, what goes into throwing a tea party, says Singer, "You make your cookies out of Play-Doh." "You set the table, then you invite the dolls. You're learning to think ahead." In addition, a child might act out different roles such as a father or mother, play a king one moment, your next-door neighbor the next.

As a rule, children between the ages of two and eleven spend an average of one full day per week watching television, according to Nielsen Media Research.

As a rule, children between the ages of two and eleven spend an average of one full day per week watching television, according to Nielsen Media Research. Parents invite even more interest. "Melanie, let's see what the Cartoon Channel has on today?" one mother tells her daughter so she can have some quiet time on the telephone with her friends. But too soon, a child will learn to change the channel from cartoons to soap operas showing more sexual content than a parent could ever contemplate. With another simple click, smash-and-burn violent dramas become the focus of today's lesson. The electronic babysitter can turn on a dime, dishing out without warning all manner of programming with the flip of the remote. No one is really surprised by research findings that show that sitting in front of the tube watching whatever comes up is unquestionably undermining a child's healthy development. In addition, several studies have confirmed that kids who watch a lot of TV are less likely to play imaginatively. Researchers say that prolonged viewing seems to zap energy that might other-

wise be spent making up games and stories. When heavy television watchers do play with the television off, they can become slaves to a specific story line they've seen. "That's not
what Captain Kirk said!" they may complain when a playmate
on the imaginary bridge of the U.S.S. *Enterprise* isn't playing
the role "right." Instead, the child who may *not* watch as much
television as his friend may be trying to fulfill a different, innate
childhood drive: *improvisation*. According to the Nielsen rat-
ings service, the average American spends 120 hours a month
watching television, the equivalent of five complete days in
front of the TV. In a separate study, the Green Mountain Wal-
dorf Schools concluded that by the time a child graduates from
high school, he will have spent more hours viewing television
than being in school.

The cognitive and social maturity of children at the time of
viewing is the critical variable in the effect that television will
have. Their level of comprehension of what is happening and
their own behavioral controls are in a constant process of development. The fact that younger children do not adequately
understand much of what they see means that they are more
likely to be affected by specific aspects, such as more salient
aggressive acts, whereas issues such as justification for those
acts may be lost. In addition, although adults can distance
themselves from violent television programs, young children
feel very involved and see the images as real. You can think of
developmental maturity and capability this way: a ten-year-
old can easily drive a car, but the question is does he have the
maturity to make the right decisions while doing so? I hardly
think so. Young children are more likely to imitate aggression

because they do not understand the consequences of that behavior as well as older children and adults do. These factors become especially important when one considers that children frequently watch programs that are not child-oriented but, rather, are intended for an adult audience.

Family attitudes toward aggression vary across the board. Children whose parents are less concerned about the effects of television violence show a stronger preference for violent shows and are least likely to learn critical viewing skills. Children from such backgrounds make less cognitive progress, are more suspicious and fearful, and show less imagination and more aggression than other children, and they exhibit poor behavioral adjustment in school. Television may also add to children's restlessness and moodiness by inducing negative emotional reactions such as anger, fear, and sadness.

Family attitudes toward aggression vary across the board. Children whose parents are less concerned about the effects of television violence show a stronger preference for violent shows and are least likely to learn critical viewing skills.

An early study by psychologists D. G. Singer and J. L. Singer suggested that the following combination of variables increases a child's risk of problematic behavior by early school age: a home where there is uncontrolled television viewing, heavy viewing by preschoolers, heavy viewing of violence, parents who emphasize physical discipline, and parents whose own self-descriptions do not emphasize creativity. Excessive TV watching in an environment where the parents *do not* emphasize curiosity and imagination has long been thought to possibly lead to a heavier emphasis on the imitation of television behaviors and characters as an influencing source of information and behavior.

The real-life experience of children is an important determinant of television's effect as well. As most viewers have little real-life experience with violence but much exposure to it on television, they are likely to be influenced by it. Jerzy Kosinski, author of the acclaimed *Being There,* once recounted a rather disconcerting experience he had while teaching. In a large classroom to which several seven- to ten-year-old children had been invited, video monitors were installed on either side of a blackboard. As Kosinski sat reading the children a story, he was attacked by an intruder (a prearranged event unbeknownst to the children), who rushed into the room and began hitting and pushing him and arguing with him. Cameras filmed the incident and the reactions of the students. To Kosinski's dismay, most of the students rarely looked at the actual attack in the room; rather, they watched it on the television monitors. "Later, when we talked about it," Kosinski said, "many of the children explained that they could see the attack better on the screens. After all, they pointed out, they could see close-ups of the attacker and of me, his hand on my face, his expressions— all the details they wanted—without being frightened by the real thing (or the necessity of becoming involved). It was as if they had paid to see a film, as if the incident had been staged to entertain them! And all during the confrontation—despite the yelling, his threats, the fear that he showed—the kids did not interfere or offer to help. They sat transfixed as if the TV cameras neutralized the act of violence. And perhaps they did. By filming a brutal physical struggle from a variety of viewpoints, the cameras transformed a human conflict into an entertainment happening, distancing the audience and allowing them an alternative to moral judgment and involvement."

Even as early as 1972, a U.S. Surgeon General committee released the six-volume report *Scientific Advisory Report on Television and Social Behavior,* which concluded that viewing television violence has serious consequences for children, making a child more willing to respond with aggression in a conflict situation, more willing to harm others, and more aggressive in his or her play. An appendix of the report, "Television and Growing Up," concludes the following: "The relation of third-grade television habits to later behavior now appears even more impressive. Not only is the violence of programs preferred in third grade related to peer-rated aggression in the third grade and ten years later, but it is also related positively to self-discipline and anti-social behavior ten years later on."

Whatever the final outcome of research on the relationship between viewing violent television content and aggressive behavior, no one can argue that heavy viewing of violence subverts a child's development.

Developmental Effects

Whatever the final outcome of research on the relationship between viewing violent television content and aggressive behavior, no one can argue that heavy viewing of violence subverts a child's development.

A television screen flickers at an average rate of about once every 3.5 seconds. The average American child in her first five years watches more than five thousand hours of TV. Compelling research suggests that prohibiting children under five from viewing TV in significant amounts will lessen the chance that they will develop attention deficit disorder (ADD) or attention deficit hyperactivity disorder (ADHD). Research findings, moreover, on ADD and ADHD are abundant and can, of course, be found in the medical literature. A companion line of research exists outside this professional medical community, however, and this work indicates that the frenetic pace of television, with its rapidly changing sound and images, may overwhelm the nervous systems of some young children and lead to hyperactive behavior and attention deficits. Research studies and literature suggest the following:

- Hyperactive behavior in children is related to rapidly changing TV images.
- The changing of images every few seconds strongly influences the development of a short attention span.
- The behavior of the hyperactive child represents an attempt to recapture the flickering quality of television.

If heavy exposure to TV aggravates ADD or ADHD in some children, the possibility also exists that removing TV from the child's environment will encourage the symptoms to dissipate. With that in mind, I suggest that parents not permit children under five to watch *any* significant amount of television. Young children of two or three have been found to be more distressed by screaming and yelling between characters than by a chase or a shooting scene, presumably because such loud or unexpected verbal arguments may strike too close to home and elicit anxiety that a child under four cannot handle.

I suggest that parents not permit children under five to watch *any* significant amount of television.

TV INTERFERES WITH THE DEVELOPMENT OF READING SKILLS

A child must learn to move her eyes back and forth across the page in order to read. But with television, the eyes fix on the screen. One hour a day in school learning to move the eyes back and forth cannot compete with four or more hours with the eyes fixed on a TV screen. It's little wonder that many children have difficulty learning to read.

TV DECREASES THE TIME FOR DEVELOPING SPEAKING SKILLS

Children may hear new words on a TV show, but this is not the same as speaking or hearing them live. If they are watching TV, they aren't spending time talking. Children generally start to talk by speaking single words, then progress to short sentences, then to groups of sentences. Reading to a child and speaking to a child directly aid the development of speaking skills. A child rarely develops proficiency with speech simply by getting older, and a child spending four or more hours a day watching TV not only loses the time needed for conversation, but may well also encounter difficulty becoming articulate and fluent. In addition, he may be less able to speak and write in complete sentences than the child who, it seems, just never stops talking.

The Internet

Unfortunately, along with all the remarkable benefits of an interconnected world and instant access to information, there are negative consequences as well for our young children who connect daily to the Internet. The problem goes much further than access to inappropriate sites; it is the collective influences of unsupervised e-mail, chat rooms, and instant-messaging. No parent can adequately supervise that flow of information. As one father said, "Who knows *who* is sending *what* to my child!" For young children between seven and fourteen, this can be a real threat, because they lack the critical faculties to recognize disguised threats. Kids who already find it difficult to confide in their parents find the Internet the perfect ally to ensure secrecy. Add to that a new style of short, cryptic communicating and you further alienate the natural emotional and physical context in which to forge relationships. Gone is the era of conversation—no time for that! Just look at the new abbreviated instant-messaging platforms and message devices that are available. This new language looks more like a log of a courtroom stenographer's notes than well-thought-out conversations spoken in full sentences. Similarly, talking heads, television news broadcasters, and pundits all give us sound bites, not sentences. These trends and patterns of communicating are expected to continue well into the future. It's ironic: as we become more connected to the Internet, wireless and otherwise, we become less connected to one another in how we actually relate.

How to Limit Television Watching and Internet Use

A small child as well as an adult needs time to prepare for change. Even an innocent turning off of the TV set requires a kind of heads-up news flash: "Samantha, three more minutes, then it is time to turn the TV off; let me know you understand?" Asking the question at the end serves to bring the child into the moment. How would you like to be in the middle of your favorite TV show when your wife walks into the room and, without warning, walks up to the TV (because you've got the remote control) and turns it off! "Sorry, Harry, we have to be at the Hendersons' in thirty minutes." Talk about being angry. Just a quiet, heads-up reminder asking you to turn it off in five minutes would go a long way toward avoiding that icy ride to the Hendersons'. Even if you ignored her request or your child ignores yours, the consequence would not sting nearly as much because of the heads-up notice. Generally speaking, the more important the issue, the more important it becomes to provide such notice. This applies to most situations that involve nagging anxiety about some future event. Somehow parents feel that talking about going away on a trip, canceling a planned outing, going to the doctors, or being dropped off with friends or relatives should be brought up at the last minute. Not so.

Children will adjust easier to your plans or negative views if you tell them at least three to five days in advance.

You Can Improve the Quality of Your Family's Life with
These Fourteen Suggestions!

1. Do not put a television in a child's room.
2. Do not allow unsupervised access to a TV.
3. Rooms must be straight and neat before the TV comes on.
4. All homework must be completed before the TV comes on.
5. Make agreements with your child regarding specific, acceptable programs, and specific times for viewing.
6. Videotape educational programs from the Learning Channel, Discovery Channel, and National Geographic that are not broadcast at convenient times.
7. Use logical consequences when kids violate TV rules: take away all TV for a specified period of time.
8. Discuss the reasons you want to limit TV; ask your child his opinions about the benefits and ill effects of TV.
9. Make a list of acceptable shows together; let the child write the list.
10. Set rules for the amount of TV watched each day or each week. Some families give each child thirty minutes a day; some children have three hours per weekend.

11. Discuss ground rules for TV viewing at others' houses and when children visit for play dates.

12. If your TV is on all the time, this becomes the norm for your kids. Prove that life is better without TV by enjoying what you do. (When your child thinks back upon his childhood, do you really want most of his memories to be of you sitting in front of the TV?)

13. Eat meals together, especially dinner, with the television off. (Obvious benefit: family learns to communicate.)

14. Ideally, eliminate TV almost completely!

Sobering Statistics

1. Amount of television that the average American watches per day: over 4 hours

2. Percentage of American households with at least one television: 98 percent

3. Time per day that TV is on in an average American home: 7 hours, 40 minutes

4. Average number of hours per week that the American one-year-old watches television: 6

5. Average number of hours per week that the American child ages two to seventeen spends watching television: 19

6. Time per week that parents spend in meaningful conversation with their children: 38 minutes

7. Percentage of television time that children ages two to seven spend watching unsupervised: 81

8. Hours per year the average American youth spends in school: 900

9. Hours per year the average American youth watches television: 1,023

10. Percentage of four- to six-year-olds who, when asked, would rather watch TV than spend time with their fathers: 54

11. Number of violent acts the average American child sees on TV by age eighteen: 200,000

12. Number of murders witnessed by children on television by age eighteen: 16,000

13. Number of TV commercials viewed by American children per year: 20,000*

*Published by the TV Turnoff Network, Washington, D.C.

TEN

Licensed Merchandise as
Transitional Objects

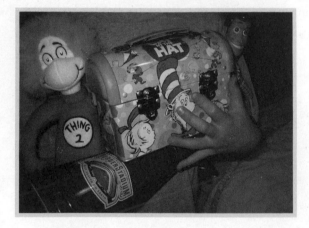

If we freely accept a child's ideas, examine them with
him, explore with him the possible outcome, ask questions such as "Then what may happen?" "How will you
feel then?" "How will the other person feel?" then the
child finds a sense of companionship in the
business of solving life's problems.

—RUDOLF DREIKURS

Character Assault

By the time this book reaches the shelf of your favorite bookstore, another blockbuster children's movie will be released or a new television cartoon series will be launched: Spiderman, Hulk, Sponge Bob, Power Rangers, Mr. Freeze, Jimmy Neutron, Barbie Mania, Green Giant, Power Puff Girls, plus hundreds more on the way. Add to that clothing lines, stickers, school supplies, sports applications, and logo merchandising, and you've got one big case of character assault.

Can a licensed character be a healthy choice for a transitional object? Well, some are. Most aren't. The problem with most licensed characters today is that they are products based on characters that leave almost no room for the child to become part of the story. The child's own imagination is in part corrupted right from the beginning. Too little is left for the imagination. Deep down, the child knows he can never match or live up to the powers of these superhero cartoon characters.

Child psychologist Bruno Bettelheim understood these principles well when he so clearly articulated that the only stories for children that provided a backdrop for real growth were the *fairy tales.* Just as the child must be free to choose his transitional ally, he must feel free to choose and change the character he wants to identify with in a story. The characteristics of a fairy tale story are all suggestive; its messages may imply solutions but never spell them out. A fairy tale encourages the child to fantasize the maybe, as well as how. It allows him to apply himself to what the story reveals about human nature. "The Three Little Pigs" makes the point perfectly. It directs the child's thinking about his own development without ever telling him what ought to be, permitting him to draw his own conclusions. This classic tale doesn't even assign names for each of the pigs, leaving children quite free to name them as they please and toggle back and forth among characters and identity. In such a story, children are reminded more easily of their brother, sister, father, mother, etc.

The problem with most licensed characters today is that they are products based on characters that leave almost no room for the child to become part of the story.

Bettelheim described the process in the case of a young woman: In early adolescence, a girl was remembering how reading "Hansel and Gretel" had actually influenced her life. When she was a little girl, she had derived great comfort from reading and rereading the story and fantasizing about it. As a child, she had been dominated by a slightly older brother. He had, in a way, shown her the path, as Hansel did when he put down the pebbles that guided his sister and himself back home. Later in adolescence, this girl continued to rely on her brother, and this feature of the story felt reassuring. At the same time, however, she also resented the brother's dominance.

Without her being conscious of it at the time, her struggle for independence rotated around the figure Hansel. The story told her unconscious that to follow Hansel's lead led her back, not forward. It was also meaningful that although Hansel was the leader at the story's beginning, it was Gretel who in the end achieved freedom and independence for them both, because it was she who defeated the witch. As an adult, this woman came to understand that the fairy tale had helped her greatly in throwing off her dependence on her brother, as it had convinced her that an early dependence on him need not interfere with her later ascendancy. Thus, a story that for one reason had been meaningful to her as a young child provided guidance for her in adolescence for quite a different reason!

When a child reads or sees most of the action stories popular today, there is no room in the story left for himself. Children identify with the good hero not because of his goodness, but because the hero's condition makes a deep positive appeal to him. The question for the child is not whether he wants to be good but who he wants to be like. Today, children are growing up with less and less certainty in their world. So, it is particularly important that the fairy-tale books and images we present provide today's child with images of heroes who have to go out into the world all by themselves and who, although originally ignorant of their ultimate purpose, follow their deep inner self. These important principles underscore without being too dramatic, the critical importance of self-discovery. Unfortunately, products and marketing campaigns leave little for children to flush in their own imagination, and instead assume the roles and behaviors that have been marketed to them.

ELEVEN

Adult Attachments

"Your father's here.
Better stop sucking your thumb."

If there is anything we wish to change in the child, we
should first examine it and see whether it is not something that could be better changed in ourselves.

—CARL JUNG

What We Attach To

I wasn't long into my research for this book when I began to confirm what I had always suspected: many adults have kept one or more of their transitional objects from their childhood, and many who didn't secretly wish they had. Memories tied to early childhood, except in cases of a dark childhood, usually bring out feelings of optimism and a renewed feeling of well-being. Last year, *The Oprah Winfrey Show* did two hours on married women who still have their teddy bears from childhood. More to the point, they keep them on their pillows every morning after making the bed! The shows were about how their husbands were resentful, and annoyed with, and jealous of, their furry little friends.

During my own interviews, parents sensed my respect for such attachments, and invariably would whisper, "I've got a confession. I still have my first teddy bear from when I was four," or "I've never told anyone, but I still have my first baseball glove from when I was nine years old." That one comment, *"I've got a confession,"* and the stories that followed would become my most remembered chapter while writing this book. Such attachments are not just reserved for the average person. Michael Deaver, an aide to President Reagan, revealed that Reagan kept a rabbit's foot in his pocket throughout his presidency. So did Ulysses S. Grant. Other world leaders and average citizens have kept good luck coins, four-leaf clovers, medals, lucky wishbones, and horseshoes as symbols of good luck.

It is not surprising that many adults delight in knowing they have their early memorabilia put away in a safe place, giving them access to their past. Like children, they need to feel safe from ridicule before they show and reveal these sacred keepsakes to other people. A very successful business friend of mine, for example, still has his original Converse Chuck Taylor All-Star sneakers, size $7\frac{1}{2}$ from high school. They're an important memory link to an earlier time in his life. Another friend still holds close to his heart his *first* leather baseball glove, which he took to Yankee Stadium in 1957 to watch the Yankees play. I could fill all the pages in this book and more with personal stories from so many parents with whom I have talked about the transitional objects they have stored away.

I am reminded of a response Professor Joseph Solomon heard from a patient many years ago who was afraid to tell her husband about certain objects she kept from her past. She said: "My thoughts are the toys of my childhood. If I give them to you, you will take them and break them." It seems that many adults who have kept a doll or bear from childhood remain unnecessarily embarrassed. Still, they wanted me to know how long they had it, how they got it, and what it really means to them.

Elaine from Texas said this:

My first teddy is older than I am. T.G. was given to me by family friends when my mother went back to work. Their daughter had "outgrown" him. I was two and an only child, so that bear became my best friend and protector from "things that go bump in the night." We were inseparable. He even went to school with me and was always welcome because he sat quietly in his seat, didn't throw blocks, and never ran with scissors. When I "outgrew" him at age eleven, my wise mother wrapped him in a soft quilt and let him hibernate on a closet shelf until I was mature enough to appreciate him once again. I have been part of many tragedies. T.G. has never failed to make me feel that somehow everything would be okay.

No one who ever suffered a staggering loss needs reminding of how their life was before that tragedy. When an event is life changing, you don't get over it, just through it. Finding and holding on to just the right keepsake can be the antidote for that moment's woes. Favorite objects pull us back to a place and time of great solace and memory.

As we seek to understand our children, we would be wise to look to our own attachments for important clues to understanding theirs. Today's cell phones, pagers, PDAs, and laptops easily fall into the category of our own transitional objects. All of us know many people who feel anxious if they forget their cell phone or pager, or about "being out of pocket or cell range" for even a quick trip to the corner for a cup of coffee. This overwhelming feeling of being disconnected is reminiscent of that of a child away from his mother.

What about when we plan a trip? What objects do we take

with us to make ourselves feel more comfortable and safe? Many travelers will remember to take their favorite music, watch, T-shirts, sunglasses, or fifty other kinds of objects that make them feel good about themselves. These things not only offer familiarity, but, more important, define identity. Our own transitional objects remind us that things will be okay if and when life becomes too stressful. Not being able to let go usually indicates a desire to connect to a secure base figure. The next time your child asks for his favorite Beanie Baby just before going to sleep and you tell him no because you are too tired to find it, think about your own ritual attachments and habits. How about what most people do with their pillow to get it "just right" before being able to go to sleep? You shape it, position it, even smell it in a certain way before closing your eyes for the night.

Surprisingly, many people are stunned when they learn the role money plays as a transitional object. We all know people who attach to material relationships with greater loyalty than to human relationships. Money is the ultimate feel-good security blanket, and why not? To a much lesser degree, our chewing gum, pipes, cigars, and cigarettes (although very satisfying) are reminiscent of our early childhood pacifier habits.

The $176,000 Teddy Bear

The adult-toy-collector market really began in 1974, when Beverly Port, an American doll maker, presented Theodore B. Bear at a doll collectors' show. The next year, Ms. Port presented a slide show she had created about teddy bears for the

United Federation of Doll Clubs. That show quickly became a sensation. This increased appreciation it excited for the teddy bear as an adult collectible increased the value of antique teddy bears. The current record price fetched for one teddy bear is reportedly $176,000. That single bear was sold at Christie's auction house in 1994. To date, collectors have purchased over $475 million worth of teddy bears in the United States alone. Those aren't all for kids. So the next time you are about to tell your child that she's too old, you may want to reconsider.

Unhealthy Attachments

Unfortuantely, not all attachments are as healthy and fun as teddy bears. Unhealthy attachments mask themselves in the form of addictions and are a sobering reminder of lost innocence. Unbroken early-childhood patterns can be seen in a variety of adult behaviors manifesting in self-destructive relationships with some of the all-too-popular mortal enemies of human nature: overeating, drugs, and alcohol abuse. Like all self-defeating behavior, when such attachments continue too long, they ultimately fracture the healthy personal and business relationships we've worked so hard to build. And while most readily acknowledge the dangers of adopting drugs or alcohol as transitional objects, many people are caught off guard when they realize the force inherent in these dangerous attachments.

For many, food too can become an embarrassing transitional attachment and addiction, becoming, in effect, a substitute for what is lacking in their personal life. Emotional eating in times of stress replaces the natural rhythm of three squares a day. Rarely do overeaters eat because they are hungry: they eat because they are hungry for what they have come to believe they cannot have either emotionally or physically. This applies to other habits as well, including compulsive shopping and Internet addiction. The problem arises when habit rules self-control.

Common Attachments

On a less harmful note, even the ritualistic routine of having that *first* cup of coffee in the morning falls under this definition. For some, missing that first morning taste of java means the immediate onset of a lethal feeling of moodiness. Just holding the cup creates a feeling of well-being.

One population that seems to be under the radar in terms of retrieving early-childhood security are the elderly. It is by no means a coincidence that elderly people, like small children, need ritual and sameness (especially in the morning and the evening) to reflect the feeling of security in their lives. Dozing off every night like clockwork while watching a favorite television show; eating breakfast, lunch, and dinner at a precise time; and not being late to places they need to be are all reminders they are doing well and all is fine. Many people are caught off guard when food is identified as a possible transitional object.

This behavior becomes even more clear when an elderly person falls sick with a cold or must stay in his house. Even if he doesn't have a running nose, you can watch his fragile fingers *clutching* a white tissue for hours at a time the way a child will clutch her blanket when she is out of sorts.

Transitional phenomena can be anything material, familiar, or even an ideology to hold on to. Religion falls into this category. When faced with a painful event, a joyous uncertain challenge, or our everyday search for life's meaning, the comfort in belief in a power greater than ourselves can be found in our heart, as well as in our religion and religious artifacts. Rabbi David J. Wolpe puts it this way: "Religion helps us cope with loss. It encourages memory and gives us rituals to express grief that sometimes lies too deep for words."

Millions of people walk around each day wearing their religious symbols or posting them in their homes, offices, and cars serving as a reminder that things will work out. Closeness with God is our healthiest ongoing transitional relationship. Regardless of faith, each religion makes available to us significant symbols to which we attach. Holding tightly to that faith, and faith alone, leads believers through the pitch-black darkness to emerge facing the light of day.

Ted Koppel recently wrote a profile story for ABC news about our 3rd Infantry Division in Kuwait and made note "that many of our brave soldiers carry with them whatever they'll need—including some special items that are definitely not issued by the Pentagon." Among these special items were a flat heart with a poem inscribed, a small book of psalms, and a lucky charm that is kept safe from the sand in a ziplock bag. Another soldier carried his girlfriend's teddy bear in his left cargo pocket.

In another story, one of the other major news programs pro-
filed men and women in our military. With no apologies
made, these great warriors opened their footlockers and revealed personal artifacts, religious symbols, old photographs,
lockets, and a rabbit's foot, all reminders they kept of an earlier
and safer time. Even among the fiercest fighters was the need
to connect to a special memory, victory, and feeling of well-
being.

If this seems too sentimental or unbelievable, I suggest reading the book *The Things They Carried* by Vietnam veteran Tim
O'Brien. The book's title refers not to the standard issue a
soldier has to carry, but to the one or two private objects he
packs to take into battle. Human nature does not change, even
in war.

TWELVE

Save Your Child's Transitional Objects and Keepsakes

It is only in playing that the individual child is able to be creative and to use the whole personality, and it is only in being creative that the individual discovers the self.

—D. W. WINNICOTT

M any parents, in an impulsive effort to shorten the stage of their child's dependency on a transitional object, may prematurely take the opportunity of hiding or throwing out their child's favorite stuffed animal, toy, or blanket. Their rationale is "out of sight, out of mind." However, parents should *never* prematurely throw away or hide their child's transitional object behind the child's back. Aside from it being plain sneaky, it shows a complete lack of respect for what the child has identified as important to him. Parents who think such moments are no big deal would be better served by thinking twice about this hide-and-sneak approach.

However, when the time does come for a child to naturally retire his favorite little cuddly or favorite object, it is a wise parent who is prepared with a special box or keepsake chest to save them in. A great source for this is treasurekeepsakes.com/gift. Such action is for two reasons. First, to the extent that your child has the need to revisit her own babyhood/toddlerhood, those memories will more easily accessed. With such a chest, she can see, hold, play with, or dress up in those early object attachments. Life has a way of surprising all of us, and won't you be glad when for specific psychological reasons your child can find their chest of favorite memories. Second, it is very common for children to regress during times when there is high-conflict family discord, divorce, or a new baby brother or sister on the way. Your child will look to you to help remind her of the kind of things she did and had when she was very young and feeling more important and safe. Bringing out that old tattered blanket or bear in a family setting is a reassuring physical symbol that she once had the same things as her new little baby brother has now. It will also signal a sign of deep respect that *you* have not forgotten those memories either. Supporting that reassurance, I also advise going through family photo albums and recalling individual great family moments out loud. This avenue of expression provides reassurance and release of pent-up anxieties.

One hundred hears ago, bronzing a child's baby shoes was a parent's way to reconnect with his or her past. While this is perfectly natural, it leaves little room for the child to connect, since the shoes hold no personal memory or attachment for him or her. Twenty plus years from now, I can assure you, your child will thank you for saving his favorite transitional object. I strongly suggest buying one of those sturdy cardboard keepsake trunks or plastic bins and filling it with your child's favorite things while he is growing up. Keep it limited and special. In it can be anything from his first robe to a winter jacket, a favorite toy, baseball glove, storybook, and of course his first blanket, doll, or cloth diaper. By the way, don't feel too self-conscious about continuing this ritual right through junior high, high school, or even college. There is nothing wrong with your child finding his or her own varsity sweatshirts, school play rosters, girl scout or boy scout uniforms or prom night photos twenty years later!

THIRTEEN

A Summary of Child-Guidance Principles

Treat a child as though he is the person he is
capable of becoming.

—Haim Ginott

Eleven Reminders for Raising Children

1. Use a quiet voice when talking. Do not scream from room to room.
2. Use few words and make them count. Don't nag, moralize, or lecture.
3. Try to be at eye level with a child when talking. This may mean squatting or being on one knee.
4. Never discuss a child in his presence unless what you say is positive and encouraging to him.
5. Don't make a moment into an event.
6. Anticipate problems in order to avoid them. This is a highly developed skill and will improve as you gain knowledge of each individual child.
7. Avoid stern punishment and lecturing. Always be certain a child knows and understands why his behavior is not acceptable. Never express rejection of the child—just of the behavior.
8. Always talk with respect even as you enforce the consequence.
9. When disturbing and angry outbursts occur, try to remove the child from the situation. It is difficult to calm a child down in front of strangers or other family members. This

only embarrasses the child and upsets your other children as well.

10. Always avoid belittling a child no matter what his behavior is like. Sarcasm and/or belittling a child in front of strangers or in front of his own family will cause embarrassment and resentment on the part of the child. He will likely plan for retaliation later.

11. Do not allow tattletale behavior. Teach that we tell only if someone is hurt or needs help. Teach stand-up behavior.

Bibliography

Ainsworth, M. D., and M. Boston. "Psycho-Diagnostic Assessments of a Child After Prolonged Separation in Early Childhood." *British Journal of Medical Psychology,* 1952.

Ainsworth, M. D., and J. Bowlby. "Research Strategy in the Study of Mother-Child Separation." *Courr. Cent. Int. Enf.,* 1954.

Ainsworth, M. D. "Attachment and Dependency: A Comparison." In *Attachment and Dependency,* edited by J. L. Gewirtz. Washington, D.C.: V. H. Winston, 1972.

————. "The Development of Infant-Mother Interaction Among the Ganda." In *Determinants of Infant Behavior,* vol. 2, edited by B. M. Foss. New York: John Wiley, 1963.

————. "The Effects of Maternal Deprivation: A Review of Findings and Controversy in the Context of Research Strategy." In *Deprivation of Maternal Care: A Reassessment of Its Effects.* World Health Organization Public Health Papers No. 14. Geneva, Switz.: World Health Organization, 1962.

Ainsworth, M.D.S. "Attachment as Related to Mother-Infant Interaction." In *Advances in the Study of Behaviour.* New York: Academic Press, 1979.

————. In "Attachment: Retrospect and Prospect." *The Place of Attachment in Human Behaviour,* edited by C. M. Parkes and J. Stevenson-Hinde. New York: Basic Books, 1982.

Ainsworth, M. D., M. C. Blehar, E. Waters, and S. Wall. *"Patterns of Attach-*

ment: A Psychological Study of the Strange Situation." Hillsdale, N.J.: Lawrence Erlbaum Associates, 1978.

Axline, Virginia. *Dibs: In Search of Self.* New York: Ballantine, 1969.

Belsky, J., M. Robine, and D. G. Taylor. "The Pennsylvania Infant and Family Development Project III: The Origins of Individual Differences in Infant-Mother Attachment: Maternal and Infant Contributions." *Child Development,* 1984.

Bernal, J. "Crying During the First 10 Days of Life and Maternal Responses." *Dev. Med. Child Neurol.,* 1972.

Bettelheim, Bruno. *The Empty Fortress: Infantile Autism and the Birth of the Self.* New York: The Free Press, 1967.

Bowlby, J. *Attachment and Loss, vol. 1: Attachment.* New York: Basic Books, 1969.

————. *Attachment and Loss, vol. 2: Separation: Anxiety and Anger.* New York: Basic Books, 1973.

————. *Attachment and Loss, vol. 3: Loss: Sadness and Depression.* New York: Basic Books, 1980.

————. "The Making and Breaking of Affectional Bonds." *British Journal of Psychiatry,* 1977.

————. "The Nature of a Child's Tie to His Mother." *International Journal of Psychoanalysis,* 1958.

————. "Separation Anxiety." *International Journal of Child Psychoanalysis,* 1960.

Bowlby, J., and C. M. Parkes. "Separation and Loss." In *International Yearbook of Child Psychiatry and Allied Professions,* vol. 1: *The Child in His Family,* edited by E. J. Anthony and C. Koupernik. New York: John Wiley, 1970.

Brazelton, T. B., E. Tronich, L. Adamson, H. Als, and S. Wise. "Early Mother-Infant Reciprocity." In *Ciba Foundation Symposium 33; Parent-Infant Interaction.* Amsterdam: Amsterdam Associated Scientific Publishers, 1975.

Bretherton, I., and M. D. S. Ainsworth. "Responses of One-Year-Olds to a Stranger in a Strange Situation." In *The Origins of Fear,* edited by M. Lewis and L. A. Rosenblum. New York: John Wiley, 1974.

Bridges, K. M. B. *The Social and Emotional Development of the Pre-school Child.* London: Kegan, Paul, 1932.

Casler, L. "Maternal Deprivation: A Critical Review of the Literature." *Monogr. Soc. Res. Child Dev.,* 1961.

Clarke, A. M., and A. D. B. Clarke. *Early Experience: Myth and Evidence.* London: Open Books, 1976.

DeLozier, Pauline P. "Attachment and Maternal Depression." In *The Place of Attachment in Human Behaviour,* edited by C. M. Parkes and J. Stevenson-Hinde. New York; Basic Books, 1982.

Erikson, E. H. *Childhood and Society.* Harmondsworth, Eng.: Penguin Books, 1965.

Farran, D. C., and C. T. Ramey. "Infant Day Care and Attachment Behaviour Towards Mothers and Teachers." *Child Development,* 1977.

Fox, N. "Attachment of Kibbutz Infants to Mother and Metapelet." *Child Development,* 1977.

Fraiberg, S. H. "Blind Infants and Their Mothers: An Examination of the Sign System." In *The Effect of the Infant on Its Caregiver,* edited by M. Lewis and L. A. Rosenblum. New York: John Wiley, 1974.

Ginott, Haim. *Between Parent and Child.* New York: Avon, 1969.

Graham, P., M. Rutter, and S. George. "Temperamental Characteristics as Predictors of Behaviour Disorders in Children." *American Journal of Orthopsychiatry,* 1973.

Grossmann, K., and K. Grossman. "Parent-Infant Attachment Relationships in Bielefeld: A Research Note." In *Behavioural Development: The Bielefeld Interdisciplinary Project,* edited by K. Immelmann et al. New York: Cambridge University Press, 1981.

Harlow, H. F. "The Development of Affectional Patterns in Infant Monkeys." *In Determinants of Infant Behaviour,* vol. 1, edited by B. M. Foss. New York: John Wiley, 1961.

Harlow, H. F., and G. Griffin. "Induced Mental and Social Deficits in Rhe-

sus Monkeys." In *The Biosocial Basis of Mental Retardation,* edited by
S. F. Osler and R. E. Cooke. Baltimore, Md.: John Hopkins Press,
1965.

Harlow, H. F., and M. K. Harlow. "The Affectional Systems." In *Behaviour of
Non-human Primates,* vol. 2, edited by A. M. Schrier, H. F. Harlow, and
F. Stollnitz. New York and London: Academic Press, 1965.

———. "Developmental Aspects of Emotional Behaviour." In *Physiological
Correlates of Emotion,* edited by P. Black. New York: Academic Press,
1970.

———. "Effects of Various Mother-Infant Relationships on Rhesus Monkey Behaviour." *Determinants of Infant Behaviour,* edited by B. M. Foss.
London: Methuen, 1969.

Harlow, H. F., and R. R. Zimmermann. "Affectional Responses in the Infant Monkey." *Science,* 1959.

Kagan, J. "Acquisition and Significance of Sex Typing and Sex Role
Identity." In *Review of Child Development Research,* edited by M. L.
Hoffman and L. W. Hoffman. New York: Russell Sage Foundation,
1964.

Lamb, M. E. "Father-Infant and Mother-Infant Interaction in the First Year
of Life." *Child Development,* 1977.

Landreth, Garry. *Play Therapy: The Art of the Relationship.* Bristol, Pa.: Accel-
erated Development, 1991.

Leach, Penelope. *Your Baby and Child: From Birth to Age Five.* New York:
Alfred A. Knopf, 1997.

Lehman, E. B., B. E. Arnold, and S. L. Reeves. "Attachment to Blankets,
Teddy Bears, and Other Nonsocial Objects: A Child's Perspective." *The
Journal of Genetic Psychology,* 1995.

Lehman, E. B., B. E. Arnold, S. L. Reeves, and A. Steier. "Maternal Beliefs
About Children's Attachment to Soft Objects." *American Journal of
Orthopsychiatry,* 1996.

Lehman, E. B., S. A. Denham, M. H. Moser, and S. L. Reeves. "Soft Object
and Pacifier Attachments in Young Children: The Role of Security of Attachment to the Mother." *Journal of Child Psychology and Psychiatry,* 1992.

Leiderman, P. H., and M. J. Seashore. "Mother-Infant Neonatal Separation: Some Delayed Consequences." In *Parent-Infant Interaction*. Ciba Foundation Symposium 33 (new series). Amsterdam: Elsevier, 1975.

Londerville, S., and M. Main. "Security of Attachment, Compliance, and Maternal Training Methods in the Second Year of Life." *Developmental Psychology*, 1981.

Maccoby, E. E., and S. S. Feldman. *Mother-Attachment and Stranger-Reactions in the Third Year of Life.* Monographs of the Society for Research in Child Development. Chicago: University of Chicago Press, 1972.

Marvin, R. S. "An Ethological-Cognitive Model for the Attenuation of Mother-Child Attachment Behaviour." In *Advances in the Study of Communication and Affect, vol. 3, The Development of Social Attachments,* edited by T. M. Alloway, L. Krames, and P. Pliner. New York: Plenum Press, 1977.

O'Connor, N., and C. M. Franks. "Childhood Upbringing and Other Environmental Factors." In *Handbook of Abnormal Psychology,* edited by H. J. Eysenck. New York: Pitman, 1960.

Ostrovsky, E. S. *Father to the Child.* New York: Putnam, 1959.

Passman, R. H. "Attachments to Inanimate Objects: Are Children Who Have Security Blankets Insecure?" *Journal of Consulting and Clinical Psychology,* 1987.

————. "Providing Attachment Objects to Facilitate Learning and Reduce Distress: Effects of Mothers and Security Blankets." *Developmental Psychology,* 1977.

Passman, R. H., and J. S. Halonen. "A Developmental Survey of Young Children's Attachments to Inanimate Objects." *The Journal of Genetic Psychology,* 1979.

Passman, R. H., and P. Weisberg, "Mothers and Blankets as Agents for Promoting Play and Exploration by Young Children in a Novel Environment: The Effects of Social and Nonsocial Attachment Objects." *Developmental Psychology,* 1975.

Piaget, J. *The Construction of Reality in the Child.* New York: Basic Books, 1954.

————. *The Origins of Intelligence in the Child.* New York: International Universities Press, 1953.

Richards, M. P. M., and J. B. Bernal. "An Observational Study of Mother-Infant Interaction." In *Ethological Studies of Child Behaviour,* edited by Blurton-Jones. Cambridge, Eng.: Cambridge University Press, 1972.

Robertson, J., and J. Robertson. "Young Children in Brief Separations." In *The Psychoanalytic Study of the Child,* vol. 26, edited by R. K. Eissler et al. New Haven, Conn.: Yale University Press, 1971.

Robson, K. S. "The Role of Eye-to-Eye Contact in Maternal-Infant Attachment." *Journal of Child Psychology and Child Psychiatry and Allied Disciplines,* 1967.

Scarr, S. "On Quantifying the Intended Effects of Intervention: A Proposed Theory of the Environment." In *Facilitating Infant and Early Childhood Development,* edited by L. A. Bond, and J. M. Joffe. London: University Press of New England, 1982.

Schaffer, H. R. "Changes in Development Quotient Under Two Conditions of Maternal Separation." *Brit. J. Soc. Clin. Psychol.,* 1965.

————. "Some Issues for Research in the Study of Attachment Behaviour." In *Determinants of Infant Behaviour, vol. 2,* edited by B. Foss. London: Methuen, 1963.

Schaffer, H. R., and P. E. Emerson. "The Development of Social Attachments in Infancy." *Monog. Soc. Res. Child Dev.,* 1964.

Singer, D. G. and J. L. Singer. "Developing Critical Viewing Skills and Media Literacy in Children." *American Journal of Orthopsychiatry,* 1976.

————. "Family Television Viewing Habits and the Spontaneous Play of Preschool Children." *American Journal of Orthopsychiatry,* 1976.

Singer, J. L., and Singer, D. G. *Television, Imagination, and Aggression: A Study of Preschoolers.* Hillsdale, N.J.: Lawrence Erlbaum, 1981.

Singer, J. L., D. G. Singer, and U. S. Rapaczynski. *Children's Imagination as Predicted by Family Patterns and Television Viewing: A Longitudinal Study.* Genetic Psychology Monograph, 1984.

Srouge, L. A., and E. Waters. "Attachment as an Organizational Construct." *Child Development,* 1977.

Stayton, D. J., and M. D. S. Ainsworth. "Individual Differences in Infant Responses to Brief, Everyday Separations as Related to Other Infant and Maternal Behaviours." *Developmental Psychology,* 1973.

Tronick, E., H. Als, L. Adamson, S. Wise, and T. B. Brazelton. "The Infant's Response to Entrapment Between Contradictory Messages in Face-to-Face Interaction." *Journal of the American Academy of Child Psychiatry,* 1978.

Vaughn, B., B. Egeland, L. A. Sroufe, and E. Waters. "Individual Differences in Infant-Mother Attachment at Twelve and Eighteen Months: Stability and Change in Families Under Stress." *Child Development,* 1979.

Waters, E. "The Reliability and Stability of Individual Differences in Infant-Mother Attachment." *Child Development,* 1978.

Waters, E., L. Matas, and L. A. Sroufe. "Infants' Reactions to an Approaching Stranger: Description, Validation, and Functional Significance of Wariness." *Child Development,* 1975.

Waters, E., J. Wippman, and L. A. Sroufe. "Attachment, Positive Effect, and Competence in the Peer Group: Two Studies in Construct Validation." *Child Development,* 1979.

Weber, R. A., M. J. Levitt, and M. C. Clark. "Individual Variation in Attachment Security and Strange Situation Behaviour: The Role of Maternal and Infant Temperament." *Child Development,* 1986.

Weiss, Robert S. "Attachment in Adult Life." In *The Place of Attachment in Human Behaviour,* edited by C. N. Parkes and J. Stevenson-Hinde. New York: Basic Books, 1982.

Winnicott, D. "Aggression in Relation to Emotional Development." In *Collected Papers Through Paediatrics to Psychoanalysis.* London: Tavistock, 1958.

Winnicott, D. W. "Transitional Objects and Transitional Phenomena." *International Journal of Psychoanalysis,* 1953.

Winnicott, D. W., ed. "Transitional Objects and Transitional Phenomena." In *Playing and Reality.* London: Tavistock, 1971.

Ybarra, G., R. H. Passman, and C. E. Eisenberg. "The Presence of Security Blankets or Mothers (or Both) Affects Distress During Pediatric Examinations." *Journal of Consulting and Clinical Psychology,* 2000.

Index